HOMEGROWN CHRISTIAN EDUCATION

Planning and Programming for Christian Education in the Local Congregation

DAVID W. PERRY, EDITOR

A Crossroad Book
THE SEABURY PRESS • NEW YORK

1979
The Seabury Press
815 Second Avenue
New York, N.Y. 10017

Printed in the United States of America

Library of Congress Cataloging in Publication Data
Main entry under title:
Homegrown Christian education.
Bibliography: p.
1. Christian education—Addresses, essays, lectures. I. Perry, David W.
BV1471.2.H64 1979 268 78-21500 ISBN 0-8164-2212-5

Contents

The Authors

ELYSE V. BRADT, formerly Research and Administrative Assistant for Black Curriculum Project in Philadelphia, now directs the music program at St. Barnabas Church in Kensington, which is in the Philadelphia area.

STEPHEN COMMINS is associate rector of St. Augustine By-the-Sea, Santa Monica, California. He is chairman of the Hunger Task Force of the Diocese of Los Angeles and lecturer in food policy at UCLA and Loyola Marymount University.

JAMES E. FURMAN is assistant to the rector, St. Mary's Episcopal Church, Los Angeles, California. He is the author of *Sand and Stars,* a resource book for Christian Education commissioned by the Diocese of Los Angeles.

RICHARD W. GILLETT is director of Christian Education and Social Concerns at All Saints Church, Pasadena, California. Founder and director of the Puerto Rico Industrial Mission, he has also written many articles on social and economic development in Third World countries.

JANE HILYARD, formerly a teacher of primary grades in public schools, has worked as family education consultant at Marylhurst Education Center and as a trainer and consultant with the network of Episcopal Trainers in Oregon. She has staffed training labs, including the ecumenically sponsored Family Training Workshops at Camp Burton, Vashon Island, Washington.

JOHN L. KATER, JR., rector of Christ Church, Poughkeepsie, New York, is also visiting assistant professor, Department of Religion,

Vassar College, and president of the Standing Committee, Diocese of New York.

RICHARD M. MORRIS, rector of St. Peter's Episcopal Church, Lakewood, Ohio, is an associate member of the American Society for Church Architecture and chairman of a committee that has developed curriculums for small church schools in ungraded classroom settings.

DAVID W. PERRY is national coordinator, Office of Religious Education, Executive Council of the Episcopal Church, and coeditor of *Aware.*

JOSEPH P. RUSSELL, rector of St. Peter's Parish, Albany, Oregon, is the author of *Sharing Our Story: A Resource Book for Liturgy-centered Parish Education* and *Commentary On The Lectionary,* the latter to be published by Winston Press.

JAN WINTER, consultant to the Christian Education Program Group, Diocese of Los Angeles (as well as to various parish churches), is coauthor of *Feast and Tell,* a two-year curriculum for first through sixth graders.

A. LEROY YOUNG, rector of St. Luke's Church, Long Beach, California, has developed seven multivisual meditations produced by the Garrison Putney Studio.

Introduction

DAVID W. PERRY

HOMEGROWN: *1: Grown or produced at home or in the vicinity of the home: native, local.*
2: Produced or located in or characteristic of the home country or place of origin: domestic, indigenous.
Websters Third New International Dictionary

He is the one who holds the whole building together and makes it grow into a sacred temple dedicated to the Lord.
Eph. 2:21

A review of the rationale on which this book is based would seem appropriate before turning to the content. *Homegrown* refers to the process of intentional and active development of a religious education program in the local congregation. The curriculum of the educational ministry of the congregation is not only the printed or purchased materials but, most important, is the very *life* of that congregation. The curriculum is all that is taught about the community from the life and experience of that community.

Thus, *Homegrown* is the process of developing and carrying out the educational ministry in a local congregation. It is "grown at home" as opposed to a purchased package. Externally produced materials can serve a valuable function in the Christian Education process; but for many, the most authentic and most usable approaches are those that are developed in the local community itself.

This book was compiled in response to a growing interest and activity in the area of locally produced materials and processes for religious education. Throughout the church there is a consciousness of the key role of Christian Education in the total life of the witnessing congregation. Moreover, that consciousness is supported by a growing number of congregations that are spending time and money on the enhancement of that educational life as a priority.

Homegrown is written not as the answer nor the perfect model for locally produced Christian education programs. *Homegrown* is intended to be suggestive and encouraging of the process of "growing your own." The chapters have been written by persons who are actively involved in local educational ministry and reflect their concerns, creative concepts, and enthusiasms.

These chapters presuppose that each congregation is ultimately responsible for its educational life and ministry. Each part of the Christian community must be conscious of and responsive to the revelations of God found in its daily life and work. Because God is revealed in a variety of tongues and forms, understandable by the people, the responses to those revelations are varied and reflect the vitality of each community in each place.

Thus, in a very real sense, each local congregation (while keenly aware of its partnership and interdependence in the whole Body of Christ) focuses its efforts to be the Christian community with a unique and lively presence in the place where it is located. Each local congregation, in conscious partnership with the global human family, determines God's call and responds to it.

The work of Christian Education is very much involved with this identification and consciousness. Christian Education is involved with building community and its ultimate focus is the building up of the Body of Christ. It is, in fact, all those things that help us to respond to God's love and presence in creation. It has to do with helping us to be God's people and to proclaim in word and deed the life of the Risen Christ. It has to do with being a people of justice and peace, with being a people of forgiveness and resurrection. It has to do with being a people who hold a faith that is vital and alive and dynamic, a living faith in the One who travels the daily ways with us.

So, Christian Education has to do with programs and plans; it has to do with designs and books. It has to do with reflection upon the life we live, and the discovery of who and where and what we are called to be. It is that task that must be done, that must be enhanced and enabled where the people are to be found in the community. The curriculum is not a package, it is a life process.

Christian Education enables growth of the person in community. It is sometimes intentional and sometimes accidental. It takes place in an environment in which each person in the family can take the risk of becoming God's person. It takes place in an environment in which the Christian on pilgrimage can discover that the journey of the Way of Christ is an exciting and challenging adventure. And on that journey the roads are crowded with fellow pilgrims and Christ himself.

Christian Education requires that our focus be the Christian Community, that the history and tradition and roots of the local community be the foundation of its ministry. The roots of the Community evidenced in the Holy Scripture and the history and practice of the Church throughout the ages are living roots which bring vitality and growth to the community today. The Bible is key to the present Christian Community. The Bible is key because it is a living proclamation of the living faith that is known in the daily experience of the Community. Christianity is faith itself in action.

A group of ten people who wear Christian Education "hats" met in Los Angles in October of 1977 to discuss these very issues. These people were selected to come together because in a variety of ways each had been working in his or her local congregation, encouraging the people to "grow their own" approach and process of Christian Education.

Following the consultation, the ten people returned to their parishes with the assignment to write a chapter on a facet of the issue of *Homegrown* Christian Education. In many cases, the ten writer-educators were aided in this task by their local congregations.

The ten chapters that follow are certainly not to be considered "the last word." In fact, many more words could be written. The topics and issues are suggestive of the wide range of concerns that face the local congregation in its ministry in Christian Education. Perhaps it would be well to provide chapters 12 and 13 with blank pages, so that you can draw together something of your own experience with *Homegrown.*

The resources and publications at the end of most chapters are commended to you as suggested directions for further reflection.

Homegrown is locally grown and reflects our belief that even as God incarnated himself in life itself, so, too, our witness of life and love must be rooted in the realities of whatever and wherever we call "home." Our home is the whole creation—it is global and local, the place in which we live.

·1·

The Bible and Religious Education

JOSEPH P. RUSSELL

INTRODUCTION

The Bible must be at the very heart of our religious education program, for it is the source of our identity as God's people. The Bible gives us our understanding of how God is working in our lives, and it gives us the impetus for our response to that action. This is because the Judaic/Christian faith is not a faith based on philosophical ideas but on a story. We respond as a people to the story as we begin to see God working his purpose out in our story. Without the story, there is no awareness of that activity of God in history and in creation. Our most important role as religious educators, therefore, is to be storytellers of the faith. Our people need to be able to feel as if they are a part of the story that is revealed in the Bible. Our role is an ancient one, going back to the earliest stages of human communal development. We share with our people the stories that give them their sense of tradition and their perspective of meaning and power in the world.

But the stories we share are not limited to the stories of the Bible. We tell the stories of the past to enable our people to discover how God is working in their own story as they seek meaning and wholeness in their lives. The religious educator's role moves from teller of stories to hearer of stories, as participants are encouraged to share their own pilgrimage of faith.

If the Bible is to be at the heart of our religious education efforts, then our people need to feel at home with the story, the language of the story and the nature of biblical revelation. They need to be able to identify their own ways of describing moments of power and revelation in the telling of their story.

THE BIBLE GIVES US OUR IDENTITY AS GOD'S PEOPLE

Something wonderful, powerful, and awe-inspiring happened to a group of slaves in Egypt many years ago. They were led from their enslavement, through the waters of the Sea of Reeds (or Red Sea), across the wilderness of Sinai and into the land of promise. Their leader, Moses, led them on their trek, but beyond the leadership of Moses these people were aware of a greater power. It was their God who was leading them and saving them. It was the God of their foreparents who made covenant with them at Mount Sinai. This people of the covenant took possession of the land of the Canaanites. They became a great and mighty nation under King David and his son Solomon. But later generations strayed from the covenant. The nation fell first to one enemy then to another. The people ended up in exile and suffered under foreign domination. But the prophets of these people, while on the one hand calling the people to judgment, on the other hand point to the coming of a new Exodus that would be far more wonderful than the first. The same God who led them from slavery in Egypt would bring salvation to the people with a new covenant, written on their very hearts rather than on tablets of stone.

Something wonderful, powerful, and awe-inspiring happened to the people who knew Jesus of Nazareth. They experienced healing of their whole being through this man. Those who bore the burden of guilt felt as if they were washed clean of their sins. The deaf heard and the blind saw. The oppressed and poor had good news preached to them. Simple stories shared by the roadside confronted the simplistic assumptions of the hearers and helped them move to a deeper understanding of God's mercy and love. To know this Jesus was to feel as if one had been born all over again. It was as if a good shepherd had come among the lost people and gathered them together in the arms of mercy. Somehow to know Jesus was to know God personally and intimately. It was to feel such a close relationship with God that the great and awesome creator could be addressed as "Father." This Jesus of Nazareth suffered the worst kind of pain, rejection, hatred, temptation, and all the other agonies that touch our human existence. And in that suffering Jesus personally entered into the suffering of every person of every age. Finally, but not so finally, this Jesus was crucified. He died and he was buried. But then the most awesome part of the story happened. He rose again on the third day and was seen by his disciples. They, in turn, received a new power in their lives and found the experience of Jesus continuing in their own lives as the Spirit dwelled within them.

These events of a people were recalled over and over again. They so affected the lives of the people that the recalling came naturally. When something wonderful and powerful happens to us, we want to tell about it and share the experience again and again. And as we recall the event, it begins to "happen" for us all over again. We find ourselves reliving and reexperiencing the event, and others feel that experience with us as we recount it to them. In time, the hearers of the story become a part of the story themselves.

But something else happened as these people recalled the events of their own lives or the lives of their foreparents. They began to reflect on the meaning of those events. The reflections, in turn, led to the conviction that God was acting in their lives and history in a unique and powerful way. They began to formulate what we call creeds of faith. "My father was a wandering Aramaean," the Israelites stated in faith. "Yahweh heard our voice and saw our misery, our toil, and our oppression; and Yahweh brought us out of Egypt with mighty hand and outstretched arm. . . ." We are more familiar with the Apostles' Creed and the Nicene Creed. "We believe in one God, the Father, the Almighty, maker of heaven and earth, of all that is, seen and unseen. We believe in one Lord, Jesus Christ, . . . For us and for our salvation he came down from heaven: By the power of the Holy Spirit he became incarnate from the Virgin Mary, and was made man. For our sake he was crucified under Pontius Pilate; he suffered death and was buried. On the third day he rose again in accordance with the Scriptures; he ascended into heaven and is seated at the right hand of the Father. . . ." The creeds of our church are stylized reflections of the story of our people that leads us to our own faith in God as revealed in Father, Son, and Holy Spirit. It is in reflecting on this story of faith that we are led to our own faith. Events happen that point us to accepting truth as it is revealed in the event.

This is the process of reflecting on the history upon which our own faith as Christians is based. We call this process of reflection theology. "The study of the nature of God and religious truth; rational inquiry into religious questions. . ." (*The American Heritage Dictionary of the English Language*). We go through the process of theologizing the events that happen to us and gradually posit our understanding of life.

Out of this process of reflection or theologizing comes an understanding of our significance as a people. Our behavior and actions are directly influenced by what we believe about life. If I firmly believe that I am a child of God called and chosen from birth to reflect the justice, mercy, and love of God in the world, then my behavior toward friend, neighbor, and even enemy will be influenced by that belief. If I reflect on my experiences and the experiences of my people and feel that my life is but an accident of nature, then my behavior will be influenced by that belief. What we call Christian ethics only makes sense as we see our ethical behavior reflect what we believe about our story. Our understanding, in turn, comes from reflecting on the events of our lives and the lives of our people.

If a story is to carry impact from one moment to another and from one generation to another, it must be reexperienced again and again. As the Jewish people gather around their dinner tables to celebrate the Passover Seder in the spring of each year, they do more then retell the story of the Israelites' liberation from Egyptian oppression. They *reexperience* the story by dramatically participating in the action of the story. As they do these things in remembrance of the events of the past, those events become a part of the lives of each individual present. A part of the Passover liturgy reflects this reality:

> Why have we just read that Pharaoh promised to let us go, and that God set us free and delivered us from Egypt? We can answer this question by recalling the four types of sons of whom the Torah speaks in explaining the meaning of Passover. We are not like the wicked children who ask: "What does this service mean to *you?*" as though they were outsiders denying their kinship with their people. They should be scolded and told: "If *you* had been in Egypt, you would not have deserved freedom." Nor are we like the simple children who are uninterested and just ask, "What is this all about?"

> Nor are we like the sons who are unable to inquire anything—for whom the whole Passover story must be related. We are the wise children who make ourselves part of our people and include ourselves in our people's story, as though we ourselves were in Egypt and as though God had delivered us from bondage. Therefore, we say that Pharaoh promised to let *us* go, and that God set *us* free.

"God is leading from the oppression of the slavery of my own fears," they might say as they share in that ancient meal. "God is leading us into the promise of our foreparents." Now the story of their people that happened so long ago is brought forward into their own lives lived in each generation. The Jewish concept of history is an exciting one. History is a living reality with the people and not just a series of events that happened a long time ago and far away.

It is this beautiful Jewish concept of reexperienced history that was brought directly into our Christian understanding of life and eternity. As the priest offers the Great Thanksgiving during the celebration of the Eucharist, we hear these or similar words:

> Holy and gracious Father: In your infinite love you made us for yourself; and, when we had fallen into sin and become subject to evil and death, you, in your mercy, sent Jesus Christ, your only and eternal Son, to share our human nature, to live and die as one of us, to reconcile us to you, the God and Father of all.
>
> . . .
>
> On the night he was handed over to suffering and death, our Lord Jesus Christ took bread; and when he had given thanks to you, he broke it, and gave it to his disciples, and said, "Take, eat: This is my Body, which is given for you. Do this for the remembrance of me."
>
> After supper he took the cup of wine; and when he had given thanks, he gave it to them, and said, "Drink this, all of you: This is my Blood of the new Covenant, which is shed for you and for many for the forgiveness of sins. Whenever you drink it, do this for the remembrance of me."
>
> Therefore we proclaim the mystery of faith:
> Christ has died.
> Christ is risen.
> Christ will come again.

The Prayer of Consecration is a retelling of the story of Jesus. It is a Christian Passover celebration shared weekly rather than annually. The whole liturgy is a dramatization of the acts of God in the past that become the events of the moment as we participate actively in that drama. That is why our Episcopal worship is an active liturgy, a work of the people in common words, symbols, and acts of praise, recalling and visioning together.

Good liturgy is drama. We are drawn into the story of God's saving action in the world in much the same way that we are drawn into the story of a drama offered in the theater. We are there with the actors. We experience the power of their lives. If the play is a powerful one, we leave the theater with a full range of emotions and commonly shared experiences. We may find ourselves feeling very much at one with the stranger sitting beside us because we both know that we have been deeply touched and moved. The drama of liturgy can be far more powerful, for it directly touches the total experience of every person. We are the actors in this drama that we are personally called into by God. The liturgy of the Holy Eucharist touches every experience of being alive in God's world, and that is why it plays such an important part in our Christian life.

As we "do these things" together as Christians, the story of Jesus of Nazareth, the story of the Apostles, the story of their receiving the power of the Holy Spirit from on high can become ours. We are as close to Jesus as we participate in this mighty act of recalling as were the disciples at the last supper. We are as close to the risen Christ as we go forth into the world "in the name of Christ" as were the Apostles on the road to Emmaus. We are as filled with the Holy Spirit as were the Apostles in the upper room as we recognize the Word of God filling and inspiring us with love and power. And so it is that we do join "our voices with angels and archangels and with all the company of heaven, who forever sing this hymn to proclaim the glory of your name." All of history becomes a contemporary experience. Though we may not feel this power every time we participate in the Eucharist, the potential is there.

Not only do we reexperience the story of God's saving actions with the weekly celebration of the Holy Eucharist, but we reexperience and recall the story with the annual round of feasts, fasts, festivals, and seasons of the liturgical church year. Our Christian calendar, in other words, is based on the story of our people. Each season touches an aspect of that story. As it is shared in season and celebration, it becomes our own experience of God being born into our lives, of sending us out as apostles and of being filled with the power of the Holy Spirit. Christmas, Epiphany, Pentecost, and all the other stories that are evoked through season and festival become personal reflections of how God is working in our lives. The liturgical church year and the liturgy of the church are the means the church has used from one generation to another in sharing the powerful story of God's action with his people. Out of this sense of participation in story and understanding comes the world view of the Christian and the actions taken in life that reflect that world view.

Within the pages of the Bible we see this process of event, reflection, theologizing, dramatic recalling and action expressed by the people of the Bible. Let's look at the New Testament. The Gospel of Mark is the earliest of the four Gospels. It is also the most primitive and least developed of the Gospels. The language is simple and direct. Interpretation of the events recorded is minimal. The writer of this Gospel was telling the stories of Jesus as they had been handed down to him.

The Gospel of John was the last of the Gospels to be included in the New Testament. By the time it was written, a whole generation of people had reflected on the power of that simple story of Jesus. The writer of John moved from simple storytelling to a reflection on the power and meaning of that story. Poetry was the vehicle for his reflections and theologizing. We are all familiar with the "Christmas story" from the Gospel of Luke. "In those days Caesar Augustus published a decree. . . ." We may be able to finish the sentence ourselves from years and years of hearing it. But what does the story mean? What continuing power does it hold for the people of God over the generations? "In the beginning was the Word; the Word was in God's presence, and the Word was God" (John 1:1, New American Bible). The writer of John used the moving language of poetry to interpret the birth event for us. That child born in quiet mystery was, and is, the living Word and power of God dwelling with God's people, bringing light out of darkness. The whole Gospel of John is a poetic theology of the story of Jesus.

The Epistles are more direct reflections or theologies of the story. Paul opened his letter to the Romans with these words: "From Paul, a servant of Christ Jesus, and an apostle chosen and called by God to preach his Good News. The Good News was promised long ago by God through his prophets, and written in the Holy Scriptures" (American Bible Society). Paul then went on to write his theology of the events of Jesus' life, death, and resurrection. The other Epistles apply the theology of the events to specific experiences happening in the lives of the people of the first-century church. The actions of the people were to be governed by the understanding they had of the story of their people. Paul appealed again and again to the story in setting standards for the behavior of the Christian communities.

The New Testament also contains the first "prayer book" of the Christian church. Buried within the Gospels, Epistles, the books of Acts and Revelations are the earliest liturgies of the first-century church. Directions were given to the people for their dramatic recalling of the story so that they could be empowered by their participation in the drama of God's action in creation. The words spoken by Jesus at the Last Supper, which we recall at the Eucharist, are brought into our Prayer Book from the Gospel of Luke (Luke 22:19–20) and from First Corinthians (1 Corinthians 11:23–25). The letter to the Philippians contains an early Christian hymn or creedal statement in the second chapter of the Epistle. The canticles, so familiar to us from the Prayer Book, were the early hymns of the church that Luke included in his Gospel. Some scholars feel that the entire letter of I Peter was an extended Baptismal liturgy, including homilies and exhortations about their future conduct, to be given to converts.

Our appreciation of the Bible is enhanced as we begin to appreciate the variety of writings found in the Bible. We see all levels of handing on the story in the Bible from the simple retelling of the event to dramatizing the stories in liturgical forms. Within the pages of the Old Testament we find stories, reflections, creedal statements, liturgies, and poetry that express the theological understanding of the people.

If the Bible story is so crucial to our consciousness of God in our lives, then it is imperative that we share the story in our religious education programs. There is no more essential task for the religious educator. We can teach Christian ethics, value formation or sex education. We can engage our people in all kinds of Christian outreach programs. But without the background and feeling of participation in the story, our efforts are rootless. We only duplicate, and with far fewer resources, the work done in the public schools, scouting organizations, and myriad other organizations. Our task as religious educators designing programs for the parish is to help our people feel as if they are a part of the Bible story. This means making the Bible a book of immediate interest and application for the youngest child to the oldest member of the parish family.

At the first level of our sharing, we simply offer the stories of the Bible. But they are not just stories about a strange people who lived a long time ago and far away. They are the stories of *our people.* We must remind each other that Abraham and Sarah are our foreparents. And the sole reason for telling the stories is to help our people feel a part of the stories, not to moralize or to teach "Bible truths." We tell the story of Abraham and Sarah in exactly the same way we would tell the stories of our own grandparents.

I feel my identity as a member of the Russell family because parents, aunts, uncles, and grandparents told me the stories of my family. Those stories give me a sense of pride in being a Russell. My world view is affected by my participation in those stories. This is the same reason we tell the stories of the people of the Bible at this primary level of sharing. If this is to happen, we need to preface every story we tell with the words, "Today, I will tell you a story of our people."

What stories do we tell? The Bible readings appointed for the Sunday liturgy provide a natural guideline for the stories we tell, and the seasons of the liturgical church year will provide us with a sense of the kinds of stories that are most appropriate in the life of the church at any particular time. Advent is the season to tell the stories of how our people anticipated the coming of God more fully into their lives. The stories and poetry that express the hopes of our people become our focus. Christmas, of course, is the time for birth stories, not only of Jesus, but of some of the Old Testament heroes of the faith as well. The glimpses of Jesus' childhood are picked up in the readings appointed for the liturgy during the twelve days of Christmas and we need to share these in the religious education setting, too. Epiphany is the season to tell the stories of the disciples of Jesus and the stories of the Israelites as they attempted to be followers of the mighty God. Lent is a time of reflecting over the whole story of God's action in the lives of his people. The readings appointed for Lent focus on the covenants that God made with our people. Tell the stories of Moses and the Israelites at Mt. Sinai, of Abraham and Sarah, of the New Covenant experiences revealed by Jesus. The seven weeks of the Easter season is the time to share the stories of the early church as related in the book of Acts. During the Sundays after Pentecost we can share the stories that Jesus told along with the adventure stories from the Old Testament.

Adolescents and adults can be exposed to the next level of story sharing. Having heard the stories of "their people," participants can be led to reflect on the meaning of those stories. We need to help our people become theologians in the sense of helping them reflect on how they understand that God is acting in their lives. This kind of theologizing leads to the statements and commitments of belief, which, in turn, leads to behavior and actions that reflect the covenant with God that we feel. At this level we will see some people come forward to present themselves before their bishop for Confirmation. Their reflections will lead them to seek the power of the Holy Spirit for an active apostleship of their own in Christ's name. But the process of theologizing should not be limited to the confirmation program. It should be a constant process included in every adult education endeavor, from the vestry retreat to the marriage counseling session. When we speak of theologians, we usually think of seminary professors and writers of weighty books. But thinking theologically needs to be our goal as Christian educators. When we help each other raise questions about how God is touching our lives and our story, we are functioning as theologians. The theology of a five-year-old can be as enlightening and significant as the statement of a scholar.

The participation in the action of the liturgy provides everyone in the church family with a sense of participation in the story. That is why the liturgy is so important for the Christian and why it must be tied directly to the religious education program. In the religious education setting we hear the stories of our people and we are led to reflect on the meaning of those stories. But in the liturgical setting, we participate in the action of dramatizing those stories. We feel a part of the saving act of God as we "do this in remembrance of me."

As mentioned above, the liturgy of our church, which is based directly on the biblical story and experience, needs to be the basis for our religious education program. If we are doing our jobs as religious educators well, we will take advantage of this natural vehicle for sharing the story. The reason the second chapter of Luke is so well known by every Christian is that the story of Jesus' birth is shared in both the liturgical and the educational setting. Christmas pageants, the making of Advent calendars, the learning and singing of Christmas carols, the exchanging of simple gifts and the host of other activities that we share in our church families during the Advent-Christmas season are all tied directly to the liturgical experience of the Christmas Eucharist. The child listens to the reading of the Gospel as the midnight hour approaches on Christmas Eve and feels a part of the story because he or she played the angel in the pageant or sang "The First Noel" outside a neighbor's door.

APPLIED THEOLOGY: A STORY ABOUT A STORY

In this section I will tell a story myself and draw some reflections about "homegrown" religious education programs based on the biblical story.

I'll call the hero Bill. It could just as easily be Sarah. Bill was a hardworking executive in the sales department of a large corporation. His goals were clear to him: He would work his way up the managerial chain of command and enjoy the benefits of increased income, authority, and responsibility. Then one day his whole world came crashing down around him. As he approached the front door of his office building, he collapsed with a serious heart attack and was rushed to the hospital. He spent two weeks in the coronary care unit of the hospital, another two weeks on the medical floor and three months at home recuperating. Fortunately for Bill, careful care and medication healed his heart and he was able to return to work. That's the experience of Bill, but it is not the end of the story or the effects that story had on Bill and his family.

Out of the experience came Bill's reflection on what the experience meant to him. "I always thought that I would live forever, I guess. I never thought much about the possibility of dying. Now I know the feeling of imminent death. I've touched death and suddenly my whole life looks different to me. The goals that I had before my collapse are not the same as the goals that I have now."

As this process of reflection is going on within Bill, something else is happening. He brings to "language" the experience in ways that can help others share it with him. "When I went into the hospital, I felt so vulnerable and helpless. I felt like the kid who doesn't swim well putting his feet down at the deep end of the pool and realizing that he can't touch bottom. You know what I mean?" Bill asks a friend anxiously. "I felt just like Peter must have felt when they arrested Jesus in the Garden! Suddenly everything that I counted on in life was not there anymore." Now Bill's friend begins to pick up on the experience, for Bill has helped her identify similar experiences in her life. If she is a Christian, she also draws on the stories and symbols of her people, since those stories form a common bond of experience between teller and hearer. "Yes," she says, "I know just how you feel. I can remember the time that. . . ."

If Bill found strength that day, it did not come from his friend assuring him that "everything will be all right." Strength came to Bill from the feeling that another person had walked the path of his experience with him. His story had been heard and his feelings had been identified with. But an even greater strength comes to Bill if he is intimately familiar with the stories of his people as they are revealed in the Bible. It is from those stories of his people that he will be aware that God is also an intimate part of his story. God can identify with Bill's feelings, fears, and hopes because God revealed in Jesus of Nazareth that he is a part of every human experience. God redeems our most pain-filled moments and fills even the empty vacuum of depression with some sense of meaning in our quest for wholeness in the Kingdom of God.

The role of Bill's friend at the bedside is the same role that we have as religous educators in designing and administering the programs of the parish. We need to encourage the Bills and Sarahs of our parish family to share their stories and their struggles. We need to receive their stories with a sense of participation in what they are saying and experiencing. "What does this heart attack mean in terms of your life style?" Bill's friend may ask one day. "You seem depressed today," she might observe on another visit. Bill replies from within his despair, "I feel as if God has left me alone for the first time in my life." "What do you mean by 'left you alone'?" the friend responds in order to draw out Bill's feelings. Through this process, the sense of identification comes.

Now let's add the next level of story sharing that leads to empowerment. The day after Bill's depression, his friend brings a gift that brings laughter to both of them, for it expresses one of the symbols of despair that they talked about the day before. And out of the shared laughter comes a new sense of hope. The symbol dramatizes to Bill that another person has identified with his feelings. The cross around her neck reminds him that Christ also identifies intimately in his faith struggle. The Sacrament that the priest offers him the following Sunday allows him to participate in the story of despair, death, and resurrection, which touches responsive chords within Bill's own experience and leads to his proclamation of hope in the days to come. Now we are at the level of participating in the dramatization of the biblical story in symbols, acts, and words shared between persons who proclaim the same faith story and faith perspective of life.

WRITING OUR OWN BIBLE

Let us say that we are a part of a planning group whose task is to design a weekend retreat for persons like Bill who have been through a recent crisis in their lives. We want to help them reflect on their own stories and the stories of their biblical foreparents in order to discern God's presence in their struggle. As they participate in the liturgical life of their parish, we want them to be able to experience the active presence of God in their lives as they dramatize their faith story.

SESSION ONE

Purpose: To enable participants to share their own experiences of crises. To build a sense of community between participants.

Reflections on the design: After a brief opening liturgy and introductions, form several small groups of four to five persons and ask them to share the stories of their crises.

SESSION TWO

Purpose: To share and reflect on the passion and resurrection narratives of Jesus through the eyes of St. Peter.

Reflections on the design: One of the retreat leaders tells the passion narrative from Luke, chapters twenty-two and twenty-three and John 20:19-23 and John, chapter twenty-one. The storyteller needs to read over the passion and resurrection accounts and rehearse them so that they can be shared as the personal account of Peter. Have participants respond individually to the following kinds of questions:

How do you think Peter felt at the following points of the story you have just heard:

- At the "Last Supper" ______________________
- Peter's denial foretold by Jesus ______________________
- At the Mount of Olives ______________________
- At the arrest of Jesus ______________________
- At Peter's actual denial of Jesus ______________________
- At Jesus' trial before Herod and before Pontius Pilate ______________________
- At the crucifixion ______________________
- In the room when the risen Christ came to the disciples ______________________
- At the appearance of Jesus on the shore of Tiberias ______________________

How would you describe the crisis that Peter experienced in this story?

What do you think the "Good News" was for Peter that came out of this experience?

After allowing time for participants to respond, form small groups and share the responses. Have everyone gather together to share general reflections.

SESSION THREE

Purpose: To enable participants to reflect on their own experiences of crisis.

Reflections on the design: Ask participants to again go off alone. This time they are to write or think about their own experience in the same way that they reflected on Peter's story. They might even trace their feelings at the various stages of the crisis. How would they describe their own crises? What do they think is their own "Good News," discovered out of this crisis? The crisis for Bill was more than a heart attack. He confronted the finiteness of his life, his human frailty, and the meaning of his life and work. What feelings of despair and anxiety remain after the crisis?

SESSION FOUR

Purpose: To enable participants to tell their stories in the framework of the biblical writings so they can find points of identification and power from their common experience of God's presence. To enable participants to weave their personal stories into the fabric of the biblical story.

Reflections on design: Divide participants into working groups. Each group will be asked to concentrate on a particular kind of literature found in the Bible and explore that literature in the light of the experiences shared by the participants.

Group One—The Book of Psalms: What hymns, songs, ballads, and biblical psalms express the story the participants are sharing together? Perhaps a member of the group will want to write a poem or song that reflects in an immediate way the life that is being shared. This group will return at the end of this session with its "Book of Psalms," to be included in the "Bible" that is being written by all the participants.

Group Two—The history of our people: Portions of the Bible relate the history of our people as interpreted by their understanding of God's action in their lives. This group will be asked to think about stories of the Bible that they most clearly identify with and to tell their own stories, using the biblical narrative as a common basis of shared experience. God called us out of the slavery of fear and darkness. He led us through the waters that seemed to cover our heads with the dread we felt. Each of us in our faith community have felt the sense of panic as those waters seemed to close over our heads. But the Lord led us out of those terrifying waters. He led us to dry land where we felt like singing and dancing the Song of Miriam

(Exodus 15:19–21). But the wilderness lay ahead of us. A wilderness filled with doubts and lost visions.

Group Three—The Prophets: The prophets spoke out of their own experience to describe how they saw God judging and redeeming the people as history unfolded before their eyes. What words of judgment and hope do the participants want to express in the idiom of the prophets of the Old Testament? "Ever since my crisis," someone might say, "I feel that God is confronting me every time I break my diet. It's as if God is saying to me, 'Robert! You'd better stick with your diet or you will end up back in the hospital!' " Out of such personal "prophecies" the group might address words to the nation. "Thus saith the Lord: 'America! The diseases that infest you are too often caused by what you eat and what you don't eat, by what you do and fail to do, by the pace of your lives and by the living standard to which you aspire. Your illnesses, my people, are your own judgment upon yourselves.' "

Group Four—The Gospels and Epistles: This group can write a fifth gospel or letters that proclaim the "good news" that participants have discovered in their own story sharing. The writer of the Gospel of Luke proclaimed the good news of God's incarnation in the world by telling the stories of Jesus of Nazareth that showed that God was truly with his people: The "blind recover their sight, cripples walk, lepers are cured, the deaf hear, dead men are raised to life, and the poor have good news preached to them," (Luke 7:22, New American Bible).This group needs to remember that the stories of the Bible are not all success stories, however. So much of Christian witnessing that we see on television or read in popular paperbacks sounds a bit like a "who can top this" game. The Bible is the story of a people struggling, stumbling, and falling again, a people aware of God's mercy and presence in their lives. Somehow we need to see good news in these struggles and not just in success stories. This is good news that people can really identify with, rather than unrealistic glimpses of perfection, which leave us feeling like failures in comparison. The wilderness, the golden calf, the painful account of David and Bathsheba, the betrayal of Jesus by Peter are all a part of our Judaic-Christian heritage because our people have been honest about themselves. In that honesty, they have seen the revelation of God. Our gospel account must include the wilderness wandering times, the doubts that we may still feel and the dark shadows that are behind the light we try to show the world. Participants may want to pattern their "good news" accounts on the Epistles. As mentioned above, Paul saw himself to be "specially chosen to preach the Good News." Our reflections of hope can follow the style of the Epistle as we share the news of our discoveries with the people of the parish back home.

SESSION FIVE

Purpose: To dramatize our common story in Christ with the liturgy of the Holy Eucharist.

Reflections on design: The Holy Eucharist frames our lives as Christian people. Let any experience of Good News end with the proclamation of Good News in the liturgy. As our participants prepare to go home, let them gather together the writings and the results of their sharing. In word, in song, in artistic creations shared, in offerings made of their lives, let the people see the presence of Christ at the table of the Lord. "An Order for Celebrating the Holy Eucharist" is the framework of the celebration. The proclamation and response to the Word of God are not only readings from the Bible but readings from the "Bible" created by the people gathered. The prayers reflect the stories and struggles we have shared all weekend. The gifts symbolize gifts of love offered to each other as symbols of the Sacrament shared this day. The Great Thanksgiving forms provided on pages 402 through 405 of the Proposed Book of Common Prayer encourage the personal recalling "before God . . . the particular occasion being celebrated." The story of our Lord Jesus Christ's and our story become intermingled in meaning and impact. With the creative expression encouraged in the rubrics on pages 402 and 404 of the proposed Prayer Book, we can include our experience in the prayer of Thanksgiving. For example, our prayer might express these thoughts: "Holy and gracious Father, in your infinite love you made us for yourself. But each of us here this weekend has shared those moments when we have felt the doubt and fear in times of crisis that separates us from you. We have felt the darkness of the 'valley of the shadow of death' encompass us, and we have cried out in hopeless despair. But you, in your mercy, have sent us Jesus Christ, your only and eternal Son, to share our human experience with us. He has come to us in the doctors and nurses, in our family and friends, in this bread and wine, and we have felt his healing presence in the flesh of those experiences. He has come to us in sleepless nights, in fear-swept dreams, in the hope of the early dawning light, in the smile of a friend, and the Good News of our common hope in Christ was felt in the simplicity of those moments of revelation. 'And so we join the saints and angels in proclaiming your glory as we sing, Holy, Holy, Holy Lord, God of power and might. . . .' "

As the Sacrament is shared moments later, the bread and wine, the gifts given in love to each other, the Cross on the table, all become symbols or statements of our experience together with Christ. We've moved from Bible appreciation and personal stories of power to a "study" of liturgics and sacramental preparation.

RELIGIOUS EDUCATORS AS STORYTELLERS OF THE FAITH IN THE PARISH

The kind of weekend retreat that I've outlined above can happen on Sunday mornings, in a confirmation group, a summer camp, or in any number of other different education settings. Our role shifts from "teaching the faith" to helping persons discover the faith as they hear, experience and proclaim their common biblical heritage. Out of this common story comes a new awareness that each of us has our own goal to proclaim, our own epistles of Good News to write, our own songs to sing and poems to offer.

The curriculum becomes the sharing of the biblical story at every age level. It means designing experiences in which persons can get in touch with their own reflected-upon stories. It means enabling them to translate their stories into words, symbols, and liturgical acts that condense and reinforce the story so that it can be seen in the light of our common story in Christ. It means that every action of their lives in the future is shaped by their understanding of God's part in their story.

Our own personal stories are woven into the common fabric of our people's story. No experience that we have in our lives lies outside the warp of our common heritage. God is with us, too. We are his people and he is our God. The sickness and death that I dread, the guilt that I feel, the joy that comes in moments of intensity, the passion of life that comes bubbling to the surface are not isolated events that set me apart, drifting in isolation and fear. They are all a part of the common story in faith that binds me to God and points to a common hope of life and peace in the Kingdom of God.

BIBLIOGRAPHY

Bettelheim, Bruno. *The Uses of Enchantment.* New York: Alfred A. Knopf, 1976.

Bettelheim's book is now published in paperback and is widely quoted. Bruno Bettelheim traces the psychological implications of fairy tales. His book helps us to appreciate the power of the story. The stories of the Bible also have deep psychological implications that we need to appreciate and be aware of. Though Bettelheim deals specifically with fairy tales, his concepts are of interest to the biblical storyteller too.

Fuller, Reginald H. *Preaching the New Lectionary: The Word of God for the Church Today.* Collegeville, Minn.: The Liturgical Press.

This is the best brief, comprehensive liturgical commentary I've seen and the best week-by-week resource book for the educator. I consider it *essential* for the religious education library (Roman Catholic). This book will help the educator see the stories that are coming up in the lectionary and appreciate their impact.

Harrell, John and Mary. *A Storyteller's Treasury.* Box 9006, Berkeley, Calif. 94709: 1977. Sold only by direct mail.

In one convenient volume are collected such individual classic tales as "Androcles and the Lion," "St. Francis and the Wolf," and "The Juggler of Notre Dame." To these are added lesser-known but equally meaningful stories that will intrigue old and young alike. The collection of forty-four masterpieces ranges over five thousand years and represents most major cultures. Whether the stories are told or simply read aloud, they will delight and reward.

Harrell, John and Mary. *To Tell of Gideon.* Box 9006, Berkeley, Calif. 94709: 1975. Sold only by direct mail.

Combining theological and psychological insights into storytelling and practical how-to steps in the art, this book is unique. Critics call it a gem, a work of art in itself. It is not merely a print piece but has fold-out pages of photo essays and a thirteen-minute recording of three storytellers in actual sessions with groups of primary age to a family congregation. It is written for teachers, preachers and liturgists as well as persons with a special vocation to be storyteller.

Pregnall, William S. *Laity and Liturgy: A Handbook for Parish Worship.* New York: Seabury Press, 1975.

As the title suggests, a resource book for those involved in planning the parish liturgy. The book provides a good overview of the liturgy, the church seasons and sacraments, with suggestions for the parish liturgical planning group.

·2·

The Parish as Educational Community

BY JOHN L. KATER, JR.

Like many young curates, I spent my first five years in the ordained ministry agonizing annually over the problem of staffing a modest church school. I couldn't really blame anyone for declining to be exiled to a dark undercroft with their friends' children, none of whom seemed anxious to emulate the child Jesus in the Temple. What bothered me—and bothers me still—is the *reason* for saying "no" that I heard most often: "I couldn't teach anybody—I don't know enough about Christianity."

To hear them talk, you would think they were lukewarm hangers-on, or worse. But, in fact, the congregations I have served have brought me in daily contact with a whole churchful of people who are trying very hard to live as Christians in a confusing and often painful world. I see them coping with grief and comforting one another; facing old age, loneliness, serious illness, family problems with courage and wisdom; standing up for justice in our city when it would be easier to remain silent; reaching out to the broken; praying for one another; bearing one another's burdens; and in countless ways testifying to the concrete reality of their faith in the Lord of Easter. Yet these are the very people who used to tell me they were unable to communicate "the Faith."

Implicit in that response is a very significant attitude about faith and education. It indicates that many committed and articulate laypeople consider themselves to lack not only teaching skills (which could be learned) but *knowledge* about "the Faith." They understand the nature of Christian faith not as an attitude or a life-style or a commitment but as a body of knowledge that can be written down, memorized, and recited at will. What's worse, this deposit of faith seems to include the whole of the Bible, the

Creeds and twenty centuries of Church history. No wonder people don't feel as if they "know enough"!

WHAT IS CHRISTIAN EDUCATION?

I believe that many of our most profound difficulties with Christian education at the parish level begin with an abstract, unreal (and unrealistic) understanding of the nature of Christian faith. We enshrine the Creeds, the Scripture, and Christian history as if they had a life of their own, when, in fact, Christian faith is *the affirmation of what the Christian family really believes:* the trusts and hopes and dreams that you and I share with the rest of the family of God.

If this is true, then the first place to look, if we want to discover the nature of Christian faith, isn't in any document or book but in the common experience of the parish family. When we do examine our corporate experience, we discover that all of us—clergy and laity, children and adults, adolescents and senior citizens—belong on a spectrum of faith that runs all the way from the unexamined wonder of a child to the mature wisdom of a faith made venerable by decades of testing. That spectrum includes also the first probing of a teen-ager's questions and the agony of doubt. Faith is no more a state to be achieved than it is a body of knowledge to be digested. Different patterns of life, varying conditions and crises, the demands and expectations laid upon us from time to time all call forth different styles of faith. What is appropriate at one moment in our life may be inadequate for us ten years later. In other words, faith as it is experienced by members of the Christian family grows and matures. None of us has "arrived," none of us has "graduated." Rather, each of us is a pilgrim, seeking an understanding and a style of commitment that calls forth our best, that answers our deepest longings and that touches us with the reality to which we give the name of God. From this perspective, Christian education is the process by which the whole Christian family shares its life with one another, nurturing each other, helping one another to move ever more deeply into life with God and with each other. Each of us has rich resources to share with one's brothers and sisters. The challenge is to discover them and to find ways to offer them to one another.

FOCUSING ON THE PARISH

It is probably clear that I understand the Christian parish to be a community in which everyone is learning and everyone has something to offer in nurturing the faith of others—even if it is the experience of doubt. Furthermore, I believe that any parish can become a teaching and learning community in which the whole congregation is involved in Christian education—in nurturing one another's faith.

I also realize that this image of the parish contradicts the traditional understanding of the congregation, in which a few (the clergy and a handful of specially trained and extra-pious individuals) transmit knowledge to the many (the rest of the congregation, especially the young). In order to move beyond this traditional us-and-them model, it is crucial that Christian people discover the truth about Christian faith as *the faith they (we) share.* In particular, it is important that a parish becomes aware of (1) what the faith is we hold in common; (2) how and by whom this faith is communicated; and (3) how this faith can be deepened.

The exercises that follow have been used with laypeople of all ages and are recommended as a way to heighten this awareness. Because they require a fair degree of openness, they are best performed in small groups of ten or less.

I. What is the faith we share?

1. Ask members of a group to tell what their response would be to the following situation: Your next-door neighbor tells you that her child has just been hit by a car, but she isn't worried. "After all I've done for the church," she observes, "I know nothing will happen to my child." Problem: How would you respond?

2. Ask members of a group to imagine that an exchange student from a non-Christian country, whom they must assume is totally ignorant about Christianity, visits their congregation during a baptism or a celebration of the Eucharist. One member of the group should take the part of the visitor and urge the others to describe as clearly as possible what is taking place.

3. A discussion leader should examine the group's responses to the exercises, and challenge them to identify any common beliefs that emerged from their discussion. List these as a "common creed." Point out that those shared affirmations are part of the Christian faith as it is lived in this congregation.

II. How does Christian education really happen?

1. Ask each member of the group to choose one of the statements from the "common creed" and to reflect on how that particular belief was communicated to him or her. Encourage the group to recall incidents, people, or discoveries that led them to the point of affirmation. Let everyone share their observations. The group will come to realize that a very wide variety of people and circumstances were responsible for nurturing its faith. It is often an exciting discovery to find that religious education is not confined to those times and places where it is formally labeled.

2. Now ask the group to list all the possible ways by which this faith is communicated within the parish community. In our congregation, the list included not only sermons, Bible readings, and the liturgy but also study groups, working in community projects, and even the coffee hour and the stained glass windows!

III. How can faith be deepened?

Groups that have completed the first two stages of this process are now at the point where they can establish their goals for a parish education program. These goals will, of course, be unique for each congregation. They should be as specific as possible and written in such a way that they can be readily translated into objectives for a relatively brief period of time. All goals should follow directly from an understanding of faith as shared and communicated by the life of the congregation.

ONE PARISH STORY

As the newly elected rector of Christ Church, Poughkeepsie, New York, I was greeted with a congregation deeply dissatisfied with its Christian education program. Like so many older downtown churches, its Sunday school had dwindled, and a widely dispersed congregation made weekday educational opportunities ineffective. At the same time, there was considerable impetus on the part of a few parishioners to "get something started." Those people served as the nucleus of a task force that committed itself to an all-day meeting with the clergy on one Saturday each month for a period of six months, with the assignment of designing a comprehensive program of Christian education. The task force included a family of four (one grade-school and one junior-high child), and a broad range of ages and interests. Some had little experience and no training in religious education.

This education task force began its work with some of the exercises outlined above. Its common creed, reached after considerable discussion, had five tenets:

> We believe that God's action in Christ is relevant in our life as person and as power.
>
> We believe that we are accepted as we are.
>
> We believe that the Good News is freedom and hope.
>
> We believe that the Good News is the power to love.
>
> We believe that things don't have to be the way they are.

When it turned at last to the problem of how to deepen our faith, the task force identified three long-term goals for its work:

1. To develop our total parish as a witnessing community.
2. To develop an educational system for *communicating* Christian experience, *strengthening* personal/corporate Christian life, *teaching* and *learning* Christian skills—within the parish, the city, and the world.
3. To understand Christian faith and affirm it as essential for life in the world.

In its next meeting, the task force translated these goals into some specific objectives for the coming year. As they were later refined, they fell into two categories: *content* and *structure.* The structural objectives were:

1. To develop means for people of different ages and family styles to work, study, and grow together.
2. To provide more opportunities for participation in the church's life.

The content objectives, which reflected the task force's grappling with some of the theological issues raised in the course of its discussions, were:

1. To construct a program for the parish to explore what it really believes in terms of:
   a. the essentiality of Christian faith;
   b. our perception of ourselves as a community; and
   c. our relationship to the community beyond the parish.
2. To create a program to teach the historical Christian faith as understood by Episcopalians.

The task force next turned its attention to its concrete situation.

In identifying the ways by which education takes place in our parish, it noted that the faith is taught through formal programs, the liturgy, our environment, and our personal and corporate relationships.

At this point in its work, the task force invited an educational consultant to give them an overview of the stages of faith development that need to be met by a comprehensive education program and to introduce some alternative styles of Christian education.

Conscious of its objectives of *participation* and *interaction,* the task force decided to adopt a thematic format in which worship and education would be integrated around common themes. In its final form, our program placed an education hour between the two Sunday morning services. A coffee hour follows the education period and precedes the late service.

One concern that faced the task force from the beginning was the need to share its work, its findings, and its emerging understanding of the parish as a learning community with the rest of the congregation. It devoted considerable attention to this task. Each month's meeting was summarized for the parish through the newsletter. On several occasions, the sermon took the form of a report to the parish on the task force's progress. The vestry was kept informed at every stage of its work, so that when the final report and recommendations were presented there were no surprises and approval was unanimous. Two open meetings were held after Sunday services at critical points so that the whole congregation could make criticisms and suggestions.

The last stage of the project was to design the machinery for implementing our program. An education committee, comprised in part of members of the task force who indicated an interest in continuing their work, was chosen to perform the critical job of selecting themes for the year and to oversee and evaluate the program at the conclusion of each thematic unit. The year was divided into seven segments, from four to seven weeks in length, and based on the church's year. An educational theme was assigned to each unit in accordance with the objectives for the year. (For example, the Lenten theme is "Courage to Live as Christians.")

Each member of the education committee serves on at least one design team, made up of from six to eight members of the congregation whose duty it is to design and structure classes, discussions, and other programs for the period covered by one theme. They also select lessons for the liturgy and suggest sermon topics. Design teams have drawn material from many curricula, and have also, when necessary, developed their own resources. Finally, the design team recruits implementers, who lead discussion, teach classes, and provide immediate leadership.

The thematic nature of the program and a three-tiered structure of responsibility require more work than simply adopting a predeveloped curriculum, but the work is spread among a larger group, making it possible to incorporate more people into the enterprise and avoiding the oppression of a few faithful souls. There is a real pride of ownership involved in a program that has been created *by* representatives of the parish *for* our own parish family.

RISKS AND NEEDS

Although the Christ Church program is still new, it is already clear that overcoming the gap between an abstract understanding of Christian education and our own shared faith has been crucial. Discussion that focused on what we really believe was difficult and slow but of critical importance for the balance of our work. We found that it was necessary to "liberate" our faith from theological jargon before our task came to life.

Developing a parish education program requires a considerable commitment by both the parish clergy and a group of laypeople who are willing to undertake the work necessary to build a successful program. This commitment is often the positive side of discontent: In Christ Church's case some of the most eager participants were those who had expressed dissatisfaction with what had been available.

Although the immediate responsibility for the program rests with a small group, their efforts will be in vain unless they are able to generate widespread support and enthusiasm for their vision on the part of the congregation. It is not enough for a committee to conceive of the church as a learning community. Unless nearly everyone in the parish has at least some grasp of that perception, the program will fail. If the congregation is still waiting for someone to give them a program, it is clear that they are laboring under the burden of faith as an abstraction.

The challenge to surrender that conception of faith is perhaps the most difficult of all. Learning to grow in faith by reflecting together about our life is much more risky than absorbing abstract knowledge. Understanding the parish as a learning community that nurtures faith is especially hard for clergy, who tend to see themselves as authority figures to whom the Christian family turns for answers to its questions. It is difficult to give up that role, but the role of co-worker and co-learner, the one who facilitates corporate learning from one to another, is far more exciting—and much closer to the New Testament's image of the Body of Christ, in which *all* the members have gifts to share with the rest.

Indeed, it is that image that best describes the vision of parish education that prompted this article. Each of us has been grasped in some way by the common life we live in the Body. Parish education is neither more nor less than the means by which we are drawn more deeply into that Body, waiting for the time when at last we will no longer see through a glass darkly, but face to face. In the meantime, we learn from one another, discovering that faith grows most when we journey together.

RESOURCES

"New Life in a City Parish," *The Living Church,* December 18, 1977. An interview with the rector of a highly innovative New Orleans congregation, in which the concrete results of a comprehensive parish program combining liturgy and education are clearly evident.

John H. Westerhoff, III, *Will Our Children Have Faith?* New York: *Aware,* III, 6. A brief introduction to the concept of Christian education as a dimension of pastoral ministry in which the whole congregation has a share.

John H. Westerhoff, III, *Will Our Children Have Faith?* New York: Seabury Press, 1976. This seminal book defines the congregation as the community within which faith develops, points out the stages by which faith grows and the needs of each of the stages, and makes specific suggestions as to how a parish can be designed to meet those needs *as a community which nurtures faith.*

·3·

Sharing Life: Learning in and through Liturgical Experiences

JAMES E. FURMAN

Christian education is a dynamic part of the human response to the Holy Trinity. That is, it is a movement within a community evoked by God's life and love. Christian education is not "creating faith" nor is it "insuring that our children will have faith," for faith is a direct and special gift of God to both individuals in their uniqueness and to the church in its mutual interdependence. Instead, Christian education is a nurturing process, a sequence of situations in which traditions are presented, explored, adapted, and enjoyed with a sense that God is alive and well.

Abraham and Isaac gathering dried brambles for the sacrificial fire, the Magi turning anxiously from ancient writings to watch a transfigured horizon—these are powerful biblical images of Christian education: a combination of doing, searching, and worshipping. In these instances from both the Old and New Testaments, the vital elements are a developed plan of action, a distinct network of shared concern, a definite act of worship. Where Christian education is richest, it is true to such models, positively aware of three specific factors: curriculum, community, and celebration.

Curriculum is a time budget, a way of planning ahead. Curriculum is not necessarily a shorthand expression for a series of printed materials from a publisher, although this can and, at times, should be the case. Most important, having a curriculum is moving with a sense of direction, a systematic plan for getting from soup to salad, or from A to Z, allowing for both anticipation and fulfillment.

Curriculum is a *statement* of what is seen as worth considering in a given place during a particular period of time. As such, it can be a formal course of study, a pattern of festivals, a series of camp-outs or retreats, a list of projects to be done at home, or an agreement to discuss selected topics in a certain order. However it is implemented, a curriculum must fit the psychological and physical development of those who are its intended "consumers." Planning for youth must be in terms of real people and their actualities—not in terms of what looks good to an adult. If a curriculum does not *fit,* it will never *work*—and it can only work to the degree that it both respects people with loving seriousness and reflects tradition in all of its immense variety.

Christian education does not end with appropriation of a heritage. Christian education requires sharing life, space, time, energy, and concern with other Christians. This is more than just "putting ideas to work." It is being part of God's family, participating in the work of healing and of being healed.

Both physically vigorous and spiritually profound situations are part of Christian education. At their best, these two strands are woven together very tightly. Thus, a retreat study of the English saints is not "broken" by time taken for a Frisbee tournament, it is "punctuated," enriched by another dimension of the community being itself.

Insist on the message that "the Church is more than a building"—but this truth will never get across until another communication has been accepted: "The Church is more than individuals." Christian education must have a dimension that *incarnates* the responsibility and opportunity for believers to be a family, a united people rich in their diversity but gathered by a common loyalty. That is, there is more to Christian education than an orderly round of Bible studies, catechism, and Confirmation classes. Car washes, potlucks, hikes, blood drives, hospital visitations, choirs, and sports events can each contribute to Christian education—provided that they are consciously coordinated by a master plan (curriculum again!) supported and enriched by many varieties of worship. This is to say that interaction is more than a frill to be endured by the serious and high-minded; it is a necessary part of having a community that is self aware and open to its largest possibilities.

It is a great mistake to think that we educate so that worship can take place or that worship is always the enriched conclusion of discipline and training. In many situations, exposure to the beauty and joy of a Eucharist may be the start of lifelong Christian commitment. Chad Walsh portrayed this well in his classic *Knock and Enter* and I have seen it happen many times. No, worship is not part of Christian education because it should be—it is on the agenda because it must be!

Worship as Eucharistic celebration of God's love in action is a rich experience in any program of Christian education. The great biblical symbols, stories, and themes can be savored and entered into through creative interpretation. Heroes and heroines of church history and the concerns of daily life can be viewed in immediate relationship to a living, present Lord. That is, through the Eucharist one hears the same voice that spoke in Ur of the Chaldees, shares with the same person who taught beside the Sea of Galilee, but now hearing and sharing in a way that is unique to the sacramental situation. Much of this has been said at great length and with great persuasiveness in various publications. The point is that there is a real educational and existential need for liturgical forms that are appropriate to the various stages of childhood, youth, adolescence, and later years.

Developing liturgical expressions for Christian education purposes also involves "at home" experiences. Definite home customs are extremely important in the process of forming Christian consciousness. Forms are easily found or developed if and when a clear focus is selected. Advent wreaths, a family crèche (which may remain in place all year), Epiphany candles, house blessings, Lenten devotions are some possibilities that are quite traditional. In any case, the task is not to pit new against old or formal against informal. Rather, the responsibility and the challenge is to use liturgy as a tool to explore some dimensions of "the mystery of Christ" (Eph. 3:4,RSV). If Christian education is, indeed, seen as part of the human response to the Holy Trinity, then the Eucharist will seem a most suitable vehicle for the one who has created the world of bread and wine as the Father, visited us in full historicity as the Son, and renews all life with abundance as the Spirit.

"LAFAYETTE LITURGIES"

Lafayette, California, is a small suburban community in the hill country that tumbles east of San Francisco Bay. Once it was a stagecoach stop for the Wells Fargo Company. Today, it is a comfortable home for commuters. Lafayette churches are small, serving a community that is ethnically homogeneous but physically scattered, divided by long roads that amble randomly between the points of housing casually created by post-World War II developers. I worked for one of Lafayette's congregations in the early 1970s, a time that included two sleepy golden summers that brought with them the peculiar demands of a rush-rush vacation time.

Panic and puzzlement were both on the agenda as I prepared for my first summer. The assignment was to create a vibrant, worthwhile Vacation Bible School; the main resource was a yellowed, dog-eared (and dog-tired) denominational film catalogue. I was to select ten days worth of viewing and package it into a program for elementary school children—very traditional but very problematic in view of the nontraditional mobility and bustle of the community. To make matters worse, the catalogue's potential was painfully limited, moving from the dull to the dated, lurching from drab to dismal. Not surprisingly, the dedicated volunteers who were to staff the Vacation Bible School did not expect anyone to come to the program other than their own children (who would *have* to attend). The feeling was that it was the duty of the parish to make the gesture of offering a program that at one time and in a different kind of place would have been well received. The mood of mingled commitment and hope, frustration and tedium, defeat and persistence, was one that I found challenging, urging some kind of creative response.

A ragged grove of gnarled pear trees edged the church. As I sat in my office, slowly succumbing to the dry heat, drifting dust, and shadowed silence, a series of convictions began to form. There is no point in doing a program that must fail. Too much time is spent on *should* and not enough on *can.* No church is so small or so limited that it lacks resources for worship. Families enjoy religious situations in which all share and develop a general basis for reflection and discussion. Except for those who actually leave the area, Sunday is always available—especially early in the morning, well before the usual 11 A.M. hour of worship, before people leave for beaches, picnics. . . . As these thoughts meshed, the future began to organize: an early morning series of services that would be *for the whole family,* a program of Eucharists with a *different* Service of the Word, a time when the clergy's sermon would give way to a congregational activity.

Cars crunched over the graveled surface of the church's driveway. One by one, the members of the Education Committee were arriving with their plans for Vacation Bible School. I wondered what the reaction would be to my proposal of something quite unlike previous efforts. Eagerness and enthusiasm were what I was hoping for and they were what I got, along with a strong sense of relief, gladness that a corner had been turned. Quickly, a theme was selected: "This Is Our Father's World." Thus, the Lafayette Church acquired something new: a livelier perspective on the oldest of Christian resources, the liturgy of Word and Sacrament. In one sense, the Education Committee had solved its summer problem; in another it had launched an on-going exploration of both the form and the power of the Eucharist.

Services for Trial Use was the source of format used in the Lafayette services. People gathered, a prayer was offered, a hymn was sung, a lesson was read. Following a brief explanatory period, about half an hour was given over to a project—making a mural, learning some songs, taking an ecology hike—whatever. Finally, the worshippers gathered in a semicircle before the altar and the Eucharist was celebrated. In many ways, these services were simple, even austere. Certainly they were unadorned. Nonetheless, the mood was festive, families did come together, education was related to worship, the Good News was shared. The "sermon" was particularly appreciated as a time when all worked, talked, shared. Much to everyone's surprise, a few members who had long been little more than names on the register emerged to attend these services, valuing them for reasons that ranged from "informality" to "a great time to ask some questions I've always wondered about."

Since those experimental days, I have devoted considerable time to what could be called "learning while praying." Coming to a parish in the greater Los Angeles area provided a new setting for the "Lafayette liturgies." The new environment brought many changes. For example, the Southern California situation responded well to the idea of innovative worship forms but regarded the original emphasis on casual dress as unsuitable. Due to the structural nature of the main sanctuary, it seemed more feasible to conduct these Eucharists in the parish hall where actual gathering around an altar could take place. Again, more hymnody seemed appropriate along with an additional lesson. Finally—quite by accident—a special family dimension was added, a focus that worked well even though various kinds of "singles" (elderly persons and youth) came to the parish hall Eucharists.

On one occasion, I was looking for a capable acolyte. Visiting a family, I learned that their eldest son was away on a cross-country tour. At this point, the mother said, "Of course, one of the other children could help." Almost jokingly, I said "Oh, all of you could do something. . . ." And so it came to pass—Mr. Long assisted with the chalice, Mrs. Long baked bread, Patricia wrote the intercessions and offered them, Frank read the lessons and served. This division of labor brought with it an enormous pastoral opportunity, time to discuss worship, prayer, the Bible, theology, Christian tradition, personal faith, and concerns in a home situation. Accordingly, what had started out as a highly simplified liturgy became more complex, enriched by a varied texture of participation.

Let me clarify what it is that suggests the reasons for the creation of liturgies. Primarily, they respond to observed needs. Wiggle and squirm on the part of children soon gives way to scowl and frown on the part of parents during a typical family service. Indeed, interaction between wiggle and scowl generally turns the joy of Christian worship into a frustrating ordeal. The reverent quiet of worship valued by adults, the length and level of preaching acceptable to adults, the religious phrases and concepts appropriate for adults are not usually valued, accepted, or appreciated by children. This is the problem of current family services (an adult experience in which children participate almost exclusively in terms of mere physical presence). That which is needed is not reduction of the adult expreience. Instead, the necessity is for a vehicle that presents Christian faith so that all stages of youth can experience, enjoy, and appropriate as their heritage the story of God's love in action.

Moving away from the old model of the family service, where does one go? One reply, a reply given in the behavior of many Church dropouts, would be "as far away as possible." A more positive answer would be "to a Eucharist that is planned for children and that is capable of including sympathetic family members and other adults." If this statement is accepted, emphasis must be given to planning for children, for if a service can appeal to them, it will speak to the lively child present in adults.

Great richness is added to children's liturgies when they include adults. The value of religious sharing with significant role models need not be belabored. Again, children's liturgies can be authentic family liturgies if a whole family shares in leading the celebration as suggested earlier. All the same, it is vital to remember that whether a Eucharist is planned for children or for children and families, it is always a time of participation in sacred reality. Hence, children's Eucharist or family liturgy is never second-class, never a condescending optional frill, because it is always an opportunity for sharing Christian teaching in the presence of the Eternal Son of the Heavenly Father.

Most recently, I joined the staff of a large and healthy inner-city parish (St. Mary's, Los Angeles). Here, the tradition has long been exclusively Eucharistic. Additionally, both Rite I and Rite II of the Book of Common Prayer (Proposed) are used. The main service already includes children as communicants and has a warmly participatory texture. Most of the factors that evoked the Lafayette liturgies and the parish hall services are lacking. Still, the concept of an intergenerational learning experience based on creative projects has proved to be a welcome one.

SEASON TO TASTE

Each environment where family Eucharists are used brings with it the need to "season to taste." I have found this to be a vital principle in avoiding the rigidity that insists on one solution to all problems, one approach for all situations. In dealing with the richness of the Christian message and the variety contained in the

Church's liturgical heritage, there is little room for the kind of mentality that says, "I take a bath once a month—whether I need it or not." Nonetheless, if one is interested in successful and suitable use of a form such as that just outlined, there are some important considerations that seem to require the respect of all. There may be need to modify my list, but the following items seem to be inescapable facts of liturgical life when one is working toward teaching as well as learning in and through liturgical experiences.

1. *Learn.*

A family Eucharist must be pleasurable and active. However, it must never be "fluffy," lacking definite substance. Children value that which gives them new information, new possibilities of understanding. Perhaps even more than adults, children are convinced that "knowledge is power." Hence, a family Eucharist should strive to make some aspect of Christianity a clear source of wisdom.

2. *Do.*

A well-planned family liturgy involves action and purposeful group movement. Concrete form should be given to ideas, values, stories, and traditions whenever possible.

3. *Participate.*

Participation centers on the environment of the spirit. The personality is engaged in learning through doing—a process that includes ritual, private prayer, as well as those topics suggested in the previous heading. Above all, a family Eucharist should not create a sense of being a spectator, of being part of an "audience."

4. *Happening.*

No liturgy should have a static feeling of standing and waiting. Enthusiasm and excitement are appropriate responses to the unfolding of a sacred mystery. If the liturgy lacks movement, if it lacks a sense of something important taking place "right now," part of its message is lost. We are to enjoy Christ's banquet!

5. *Accepting.*

Children must be accepted as children. It is quite normal to be seven or fifteen! Hence, "hushing" and controlling should not be part of the liturgical agenda, although undue and obvious disruptions should be remedied.

6. *Sharing.*

The educational concept of learning through doing relates to the theological idea of shared ministry. The Eucharist contains many opportunities for participation (e.g., preparing the worship area, reading, serving as an acolyte, leading prayer, ushering, presenting the offering, etc.). These roles should be assigned appropriately, possibly using members of one family as the staff of a given Eucharist. In any case, there should be enough people working with the celebrant so that it is clear that liturgy is the public work of the Christian community, not exclusive the task of the clergy.

7. *Reading.*

It is good to have children read the lessons chosen for the Eucharist but they need guidance if they are to do this with both confidence and skill. The person responsible for helping the readers should: 1) explain the meaning of the passage, review ideas and issues; and 2) coach the reader in terms of voice use, diction, control, and appropriate style.

8. *Guidance.*

There is a vital difference between praying and reading a prayer. This distinction applies to all participation roles in liturgy. Consequently, those persons responsible for conducting these theme-related Eucharists must be sure that all involved have a clear understanding of both the overall theme of the service and their role in it.

9. *Prayers.*

It is appropriate for children to write the major intercession or general prayer to be used in the Eucharist. Such a prayer must be composed well in advance of the service. When a child prepares the intercessions, style, phrasing, and specifics must come from his or her own world. On the other hand, the structure and general format must follow the usual liturgical pattern.

10. *Experiencing.*

Skits, plays, media presentations, talks, and demonstrations by children and/or adults are all suitable for developing the teaching theme of the Eucharist. In a family, Eucharist teaching normally takes place through an action-time or process, not during an address by a leader. At the same time, a short homily or reflection following the group activity usually helps to summarize or draw out the meaning of what has been done together.

11. *Gestures.*

Symbolic gestures (ceremony), which have a clear communication value, are important as "punctuation marks" during the liturgy. They should be explained with conviction and enthusiasm. After a while, they become part of the language of worship, again teaching through doing.

As much as possible, the whole group should participate in such gestures (e.g., bowing the head, kneeling, etc.), though some are more suitable for only the celebrant and those assisting at the altar. Creative imagination may suggest new forms of symbolic expression for particular occasions, though many traditional ceremonies (e.g., handshake, hug, washing of hands, sign of the cross, etc.) will always be appropriate.

12. *Clarity.*

Since various parts of any newly written family Eucharist will be first-time experiences, it is important that the leader provide brief verbal cues. These cues are short introductions or follow-ups, not commands or admonitions. The worship leader should be able to talk through each liturgy much as "The Galloping Gourmet" or Julia Child explains a recipe while preparing it.

13. *Structure and Outline.*

Liturgies planned for children are not an attempt to reinvent Christian worship. They follow the classic Eucharistic pattern (opening rite, Liturgy of the Word, Eucharist, and closing prayers) while using creative resources to focus on particular aspects of Judaeo-Christian experiences. Thus, the structural relationship to more formal services is preserved even though a different style and mood prevail.

14. *Environment.*

Family Eucharists—like all worship—assume a setting that combines flexibility, practicality, and beauty.

> **Flexibility:** The worship area can be arranged and rearranged easily so as to accommodate the demands of varied liturgies. The place of worship should encourage and not inhibit projects and activities that require considerable movement as well as conversation and small-group interaction.
>
> **Practicality:** The liturgy must be in harmony with the resources of its setting (e.g., lighting, electrical outlets, stage area, wall space, overall size, seating and/or standing area, noise, etc.).
>
> **Beauty:** The Eucharist is a holy celebration. Its setting should be attractive, festive, and enjoyable. The altar and its appointments, the chalice, and the celebrant's vestments should be worthy of their role in liturgical worship.

15. *Music.*

Music often establishes the mood of worship. In any theme-related liturgy, it is very important to select hymns or songs that emphasize the appropriate message. They may be modern or traditional, but they must always be easy to sing and should not become a burden in terms of either textual complexity or musical difficulty. A few well-chosen hymns or songs are better than a "hymn sandwich," which forces too much on the group in an effort to fill in time or space in the liturgy.

16. *Mood.*

Celebrating a family liturgy should not be an occasion for casualness for its own sake. It should be a creative opportunity for communication of the Gospel, exploration of liturgical heritage, and encounter with the Risen Christ. Family Eucharists require dignity, prayer, and preparation as well as spontaneity and experimentation.

The Book of Common Prayer (Proposed) contains many riches. One of them is "An Order for Celebrating the Holy Eucharist." Bearing in mind that "it is not intended for use as the principal Sunday or weekday celebration," this order provides the Christian educator with a powerful new tool. It is no longer necessary to improvise versions of Morning Prayer or to put up with pathetic shadows of the Eucharist when one wishes to have a solid worship program in the Church School. Using this order in an educational context enables children to reclaim dimensions of heritage lost or obscured due to our preoccupation with "adults only" worship and "children only" education. In this regard, it seems almost astonishing that Anglicans have been so insensitive, while Roman Catholics developed a splendid understanding of Masses for children and Protestants created a long-standing repertoire of "children's chapels" (usually taking the form of sermonettes rather than liturgies, however).

IS IT ALL WORTH IT?

Is it really worth the time and trouble required to develop special liturgies for children, for children and families? Is this more than yet another energy-consuming fad, which will distract clergy and laity from weightier considerations? Clearly, these are, for me, loaded and largely rhetorical questions. Still, they must be asked and answered with some care in any situation where this approach is considered. It is, in fact, true that both can be answered "no" in some cases, for reasons of varying worthiness. However, it will be generally true that nothing has been done in this area. Where special Eucharists have been instituted, the results have been dramatically satisfactory. Adults have found them extremely useful as time in which to ask questions left over from as long ago as sixth grade (usually the last time that Christian education was on the "must" list of activities). Children have been given excellent preparation for being part of adult services, gaining a clear sense of "the shape of the liturgy." Themes of the greatest diversity have been presented in an exciting, intergenerational milieu, which allows reflection from many standpoints, at many levels of maturity. All have had opportunity to experience the content of the "big words" of the faith (e.g., grace, Holy Trinity, Baptism) and the major images (e.g., sheep in their dual dimension as fuzzy white grazing machines and as symbols of human need in the face of God's love). In short, this kind of Eucharistic education can and should be a respected part of any program that listens attentively to the Lord's imperative: "Let the children come to me; do not try to stop them; for the kingdom of God belongs to such as these" (Mark 10:14, NEB).

RESOURCES

Sloyan, Virginia, ed. *Signs, Songs, and Stories: Another Look at Children's Liturgies.* Washington, D.C.: The Liturgical Conference, 1974. *Signs, Songs, and Stories* represents a Roman Catholic spectrum with Anglican participation (The Reverend Urban Holmes, "Perceiving the Unapparent"). It is a remarkable feast, containing superlative articles of great value. The range of topics is excellent, all exploring both the theological and the "how to" factors. Stressing the often-overlooked fact that liturgy is more than words, *Signs, Songs, and Stories* is particularly strong in showing how to use words (e.g., the four articles collected under the heading "Telling the Bible Story"–especially C. E. S. Gavin's contribution, "What Kind of Story Is This?"). This book is a true "must" for understanding and developing worthwhile children's Eucharists.

Babin, David E. *The Celebration of Life: Our Changing Liturgy.* New York: Morehouse-Barlow, 1969. Father Babin provides a superb statement of what the revised liturgies of the Episcopal Church are intended to implement. Basic definitions are provided in a way that brings life and liveliness to a fundamental area of concern.

Faucher, W. Thomas and Nieland, Ione C. *Touching God: A Book about Children's Liturgies.* Notre Dame: Ave Maria Press, 1975. *Touching God* is a treasure house, which complements *Signs, Songs, and Stories* in important ways by providing seventeen model liturgies for grades one through six. The photographs are useful in sharing feeling and mood. *Touching God* reviews the basic questions concisely ("What Are Children's Liturgies?") and turns to important working issues ("Role of the Priest"). The Appendix is the extremely valuable Vatican decree, which says very intelligent things in an authoritative form.

Sloyan, Virginia, and Huck, Gabe, eds. *Children's Liturgies.* Washington, D. C.: The Liturgical Conference, 1970. Here is the foundation stone of the structure of current American Roman Catholic thought on the matter at hand. The introduction is large-scale and highly useful. Establishing mood and the importance of setting are stressed. At the time of its publication, *Children's Liturgies* was unique, a fact that gives it both the boldness of pioneering and the limitations of an early model. In general, it differs from *Signs, Songs, and Stories* in that it presents a "here are the tools" content rather than reflection on the whys and hows that relate to such items.

When the frame of reference has been established, other books can be used with varying degrees of usefulness. Since all are Roman Catholic in origin, the available books relate to liturgical texts and models that are not in use in the Episcopal Church. Additionally, if one really absorbs the ideas in works such as those edited by Sloyan and Huck or prepared by Babin, the value of the following titles is primarily found in their suggestion value, not in their ability to provide something for direct copying.

Freburger, W. J., and Haas, James E., eds. *Eucharistic Prayers for Children.* Notre Dame: Ave Maria Press, 1976. I like this book because of its analysis of what goes into a Eucharistic prayer. It shows just how seriously the Roman Catholic Church takes the need for services for children. Many of the twenty suggested liturgies deal with theological concerns not usually presented (e.g., "Election," "Care and Concern," "Covenant").

LeBlanc, Etienne, Talbot, Mary Rose, eds. *How Green Is Green?* Notre Dame: Ave Maria Press, ND. This is a very fine collection of thirty-eight Eucharists "for today's youth." Topics relate to school and teen-age issues (e.g., "Laws and Rules," "Those Tempted by Drugs," "Maturity") as well as to more traditional topics. A clear format is extremely helpful as are the suggestions provided for each liturgy. Especially in a church-related school with a strong tradition of chapel, this book should have high value.

Gamm, David. *On Cloud Nine.* Notre Dame: Ave Maria Press, 1976. Here is a collection of twenty-four model Eucharists and four penance services for grades one through four. It particularly emphasizes the liturgical seasons. Vigorous and well-attuned to younger children, the liturgies of *On Cloud Nine* are always excellent resources for ideas for all ages. A wealth of music is suggested. It should be noted that Father Landry's "Hi God" series of records is an extremely helpful resource in this area. As with all Ave Maria Press publications, there is a useful intordoctory chapter, which puts the case for children's liturgy with cogency.

In planning the "activity sermon," it is good to have some suitable source books. Two fine offerings are: Thea Eroes, *Handbook of Art Activities for Middle-Grade Religion Programs,* New York: W. H. Sadlier, 1972; and Thomas Conway and Frank J. Martino, *Handbook of Creative Activities for Upper-Grade Religion Programs,* New York: W. H. Sadlier, 1972. Each has a valuable point of view (*Art Activities:* "Life's Wonders"; "Belonging"; "God's Family"; "Advent"; "Christmas"; "Jesus in my Fellow Man"; "Go Forth in the Spirit"; *Creative Activities:* "Identity";

"Involvement"; "Scripture"). Together, this set does a beautiful job of covering important bases.

Wolfes, Betty. *The Banner Book.* New York: Morehouse-Barlow, 1974. Decidedly a book about banners, this is a richly illustrated guide to the "where, when, how, and why" of this type of creativity.

Post, W. E. *Saints, Signs, and Symbols.* New York: Morehouse-Barlow, 1974. This is a must if and when anything creative is to be done that involves the Church's wealth of symbols. It is a rich and useful book.

Modern Liturgy. A remarkable source of ideas published eight times a year. It is generally provocative and helpful. A subscription is $16.50 for one year (Resource Publications, P. O. Box 444, Saratoga, California 95070).

An exquisite audiovisual resource is now available for the rather neglected Epiphany season and its celebration. I have used this item in children's liturgies with great success. *The Star of Bethlehem* is a seven-minute, full-color, sound, 35mm filmstrip (also available as a slide set) meditation on Sir Edward Burne-Jones' painting. This is an elegant treatment of a richly symbolic biblical statement. Order from Burt Martin Associates, P. O. Box 6337, Burbank, California 91510; $15.00.

·4·

The Space around Us

RICHARD M. MORRIS

I will find my own balance
I ask only that you leave me room to grow
and to go
and to come
and to become. . . . .

And I will lead you to a special place I know
where butterflies
Let you hold them in your hair

And I will teach you
that meeting is more than time and space
and trysting furniture[1]

Somewhere in the past a building was built, and it was the dream of those who built it. It was "the last word" in buildings. They were building schools all over the district—red brick and glass and shiny new with modular furniture; each class tucked neatly into its own four walls. And so we built the "last word" in an education wing and we filled it with children as the suburbs grew around us.

And so you and I inherit a place someone else built. And now we've outgrown it; or it's too big; or the curriculum changed or the theory changed; so now it isn't suitable in any way.

Space is essential to us for any activity. Space is more than four walls: it's the world we live in—all of it. Space is not always physical—it may be the space we require around us in order to be who we must be.

---

1. *Songprints.* Text copyright 1972 and 1973 by Joe Wise and North American Liturgy Resources, 300 East McMillan Street, Cincinnati, Ohio 45219. All Rights Reserved. Written permission must be obtained from the Publisher before reprinting or copying from this Work.

Sometimes I am happy living with myself in my own space. Sometimes I am not, but I discover that I am my best self when I am at peace with my inner space. And that is an environmental observation. We can create an environment of inner space that is comfortable or uncomfortable. If I fill my inner consciousness with darkness and filth and jealousy and hate and pettiness, it is an uncomfortable environment within which to live. But, if I fill my inner space with light and love and the bright colors of enthusiasm and excitement, it is a peaceful, secure place and one that I find I want to share with others around me. Somehow I never wanted to share my dark and seamy space with anyone. Jesus talked a lot about *light* and inner space. He even said he would share that space with us if we asked. Now that would be some environment!

We share a task of Christian education, and we share some other things in common—four walls, which are called a classroom—room for a class. But who's in charge here? Who is to control that space, which is to contain and enclose a group of people?

Two churches sit on opposite corners on a village street. In one there is a corridor like a spine, supporting rooms of equal dimensions—square, clean, sterile. On the door of each room is a sign making it quite clear who belongs here: K through 12. The chairs are neatly placed around the table. The chalkboard is washed clean. The bulletin board has a very carefully arranged display of pictures, which tell of Palestine in Jesus' day. The room seems to speak, and it says to those who enter: You are going to learn about Jesus of Nazareth and I, the teacher, am going to teach you what you should know, and when we're finished, please put your chairs neatly under the table just like you found them. Christian education is taught here.

In the other church, across the street, something has happened. The people in this church also inherited a corridor of rooms, door opposite door; but the doors have been taken off, so now it's doorway opposite doorway. As you walk down the corridor you are visually drawn through a doorway and find yourself amidst walls of color and texture and things hanging and things pasted and perhaps a chart in crude lettering, which tells about those things that "we discovered about Jesus." The high ceilings have been lowered, but only visually, so there is still lots of airiness. The carpet on the floor invites you to sit and, if that's too hard, then grab a pillow from the pile in the corner. And the space seems to speak, and it says to those who come here, "This is our space where we are in the process of discovering together all kinds of things about ourselves and about Jesus, and, if you really try, '. . . butterflies let you hold them in your hair.' "

There always seem to be these two kinds of churches. In the first, we control the space and the space controls the learner. In the second, we control the space and the space sets the learner free.

I am concerned about the space within which Christian Education takes place. Therefore, I am concerned for the whole building, which houses the people of God—at worship, at play, and at study. I am concerned because space becomes environment and environment affects how we worship, how we play and how we learn; indeed, it affects *what* we learn.

When I was a small boy I had a hideout. It was a place I created and to which I returned regularly. I rarely invited anyone to visit, but some people were invited. I learned a lot there because I felt that it was mine.

Space needs to be owned, and whatever we do with the space that we have been given, those who use it need to own it. That would be my first rule of thumb, and since thumbs are all different, there is some flexibility in that rule.

Space needs to reflect what happens, or is supposed to happen in that space. It needs to allow what is supposed to happen to happen.

Therefore, space must provide some boundaries, some clues as to what the space is for, but at the same time provide the flexibility that allows growth and expression and creativity. The universal issue of freedom within discipline is true also of environment.

Education begins when a person wakes up on a Sunday morning and prepares to go to church; it continues when he or she enters the doors of the nave and throughout the service (through content, relationships, and environment) and continues into the classroom and the teacher's lesson plan. Nor does it end with the ride home, but continues in the life of the family. Indeed, it never stops.

And in the midst of that ongoing experience of learning, we spend some of our time in church space. Is it drab? Is it sterile? Is it cared for and clean? Is it fun and an interesting place to be?

The Christian faith is a happy and victorious faith. There is great joy in God's creation. Educational and liturgical space exists as a place where people can discover together the joy of God as Creator as they live out their need for redemption and are empowered by the Spirit for mission. Look around you at the church space you occupy—does it reflect the joy of God's creation?

Take a long, serious look at your church building. Now, go into the shopping malls of your city or suburb or nearby marketplace and *see* what is there. Supergraphics of color move you from one department to the next. Worked into those graphics are a statement of where you are and what you can expect. Somebody took time to make certain that you noticed what they wanted you to notice. They have created a colorful, busy place and added some excitement to your otherwise uneventful daily routine.

Really look, and now "steal some ideas" that will work for you at very little cost. Come back to the church and try *one*. Add another! Be daring!

We have a responsibility to have things clean—that is a basic starting point, whether we are talking about church or the homes from which we come. That much simply says "we care." But remember, a fresh coat of paint costs the same amount of money and time whether we paint everything institution-buff, hospital-white, or in exciting colors and supergraphics.

Someone walked into our church space the other day and exclaimed: "What a happy place this is—tell me what goes on here." She was referring to our open classroom area. Open? There are lots of walls. Yes, open! Open to children and adults to discover together the joy of God's love in Jesus Christ. Open to children who are more important than facts to be taught—but the latter does not get neglected.

Supergraphics? You bet. Ever-expanding circles of yellow and orange moving down the corridor and around the corners into the rooms, drawing you from place to place. Circles of relationships ever growing. Circles of knowledge ever expanding. Whatever they may mean to you they speak a language of openness.

Dorothy, in *The Wizard of Oz,* followed the yellow brick road—how else would she have found her way? Bands of color down corridors and around corners. Combinations of colors in different sections of the building for easy directions: "Go to the red-and-white section and you'll find what you are looking for."

The Day Nursery room has off-white walls waiting to be covered with a myriad of the results of fascinating three- and four-year-old activities. But what makes the room exciting? . . . A big square fire-engine-red area carpet that invites you to get down and play "butterfly" on your back and look at the ceiling from which are hanging interesting things like ghostly figures, because it's Halloween and the eve of All Saints' Day.

WHAT WE LEARNED ABOUT A READING SPACE

We set up an area (room) with attractively decorated walls and furniture, using library tables and chairs, with books neatly catalogued and prominently displayed.

Children in the open classroom were completely free to choose to use this room and read a book. Indeed, they were encouraged. Many looked in but no one went in for two months.

At the end of this time, between Sundays, we removed all the furniture and replaced it with an enormous pile of bright pillows and a rocking chair, a low table, and casually displayed books around the room.

The next Sunday, seven children spent their whole hour reading, and they were upset when told that "time was up" and they had to go into church and join their parents. Since that Sunday, the room has always had children in it and they have been reading.

WHAT DOES EDUCATIONAL SPACE LOOK LIKE?

1. It should be large enough for movement. It should fit the number of people who will use it.

We all need space to "be." But since we do more than stand or sit in one place for any extended period of time, we need to be sure to provide enough space for the kind of activity we plan to engage in. You can't play basketball in a room with a seven-foot ceiling, but you can play other kinds of games. You cannot do active play with twenty children in a room twelve feet by twelve feet. That would seem obvious; but then, neither is a room twenty feet by thirty feet with nine-foot ceilings appropriate for a small group of six first graders.

So, as you begin to think about environment as space, ask first of all who is going to use it? How many people will use it? What is it that we want them to be able to do in the space we are providing?

Many of us have inherited old buildings with very high ceilings. Let us remember that children are small. But since adults will also have to use the same rooms with children, it is obvious that we cannot scale everything down to children's size. There are, however, things that we can do. For instance, by adding an eight-inch piece of unfinished cedar board all around the room, so that it touches the moulding at the top of the door frame, and painting the wall above that board the same color as the ceiling, the ceiling will visually appear to be lower.

Or fasten a two-inch-by-six-inch construction-grade board on opposite walls of a room (the full length) at door height and then secure two-inch-by-eight-inch boards on edge on these "ledges" that you have created. Put these boards sixteen inches on center and leave them unfinished.

You now have a new ceiling slightly under seven feet; you have allowed the existing lighting to continue to do its job; and you have added to the brightly painted walls the warmth and texture of unfinished wood. But, most of all, the room is inviting to small children.

2. *Floors, ceiling, walls, and air space should all be usable space.* In the room that I have just described, the space is totally usable. The walls are available for pictures or other activities, but so is the ceiling, for by putting an 18-inch bar of metal or wood across two of the upright boards in the ceiling you have created, you can hang plants, banners, mobiles, or whatever other things you want. You don't need nails. You don't deface the ceilings, and you have "instant" display space. Indeed, you can literally suspend things of considerable weight in the middle of the room, including furniture. Such a ceiling would allow instant backdrops and props for dramatics, if that were the activity of the day.

As for the floor, it is meant for more than walking. People, especially children, love to sit on the floor. . . . So make it inviting with a carpet and with stacks of pillows. We can take a lesson from commercial enterprises. Carpet costs less to maintain (and ultimately to replace in eight to ten years) than the cleaning and waxing of vinyl-type floor coverings, and the space is quieter, more colorful, and more flexible.

3. *There should be some surprises.* In setting up an educational environment, especially in an open-classroom situation, we need to create some areas of special interest. If you stand at any one place in the learning area, you shouldn't be able to see everything at once. Rather, create some corners that hide surprises: a quiet game area, or a reading corner. One church built a low platform eight feet off the floor in the corner of a room and filled it with pillows and put a fuzzy rug on the floor (three feet by eight inches). Sometimes it served as a stage for impromptu dramatic skits, but it also served as a place where one or two children could curl up and read a book, or a child and a resource person could meet and share.

Sometimes people need to be alone and do nothing (which is really something!). Can they find a place to do that in the normal regimented classroom? In the educational area of the open classroom, we have provided a quiet nook, a high-back chair in the corner of the reading area and then, when it's being used, respect the privacy. More may be happening than you ever suspect if you can find the ability to let go and not always be in control of children's lives.

4. *When the area is empty, there should still be color, texture, and warmth.* We need to be bold in our use of color and imaginative in our use of materials, so that everything is not drab and two-dimensional. Take a good look at your educational space. When people walk into it—is it exciting? Is it inviting? Does it make you feel happy? We are limited here in being too specific, but combine wood, fabric, paint, plants, carpet, and *simple* furniture.

5. *The area needs people for its completion, since space exists for people, not for itself.* Every good stage set is designed to enhance the activities of the players. The play's the thing, not the scenery! To this end, space needs to be flexible and changing. With the addition of a few props, or simple furniture, the space can take on

a specific intention for use. Likewise, those things that are added to any given space physically convey the nature of the activity to be carried out in that area.

A reading area becomes easily distinguishable from an AV center with all its electronic equipment. The absence of a carpet and the existence of paint easels says quite clearly that this space is for creative activities, and the space speaks of a freedom for those who use it to make a "mess." The environment we create says to people: "You can act a special way in this place," or, "This place expects me to be quiet," etc.

Does your education space say "Come in and explore the joy of being a part of the resurrection community—the Easter people?" We say more to people than we realize by the physical environment we create.

·5·

Thematically Developed Environments in Christian Education

A. LEROY YOUNG

On Sunday, November 2, 1975, at St. Luke's Church, Long Beach, California, "The Great American Dirigible and Lighter than Air Craft Co., Ltd.," was launched. Planned as a Sunday-morning unit on Holy Spirit, the thematically developed program involved a hundred children and thirty-five adults in the twelve weeks it was in operation. Central to and visually dominating the teaching environment was a sixty-seven-foot "dirigible." The fantasy airship had been painted on the glass sliding doors that housed the five rooms in which the project took place. The enclosed patio through which the participants entered had a compatible treatment. Covering the iron grating at the far end were pressed-wood panels on which, in billboard dimensions, were simulated clouds, blue sky, and the sun. Each of the five subdivisions in the "dirigible," appropriately identified by exterior signs, reflected in their interior design and decor the constituent sections of the imaginary flying machine. On a rotational basis the children entered and experienced the activities taking place in the "Flight Deck," "Sky Lounge," the "Communication Center," "Mile-High Theater," and the "Engine Room." Locally planned and developed, "The Great American Dirigible and Lighter than Air Craft Co., Ltd.," was one of several "curriculum environments" to be used in the church since the summer of 1973.

The atypical educational configurations represented a response to a combination of problems confronting many churches. St. Luke's, a once-thriving central-city parish, was by 1970 assaulted by urban erosion. The exodus of the membership to the suburbs had left in its wake a modern educational complex and an ever-shrinking Sunday school enrollment. Fewer students and reduced class sizes forced group grading. Teachers, difficult to recruit even in prosperous days, became a problem. The aging membership proved to be a limited pool for leadership resources. Proposed solutions, and there were several, usually took the form of a search for the ideal curriculum. The belief persisted that somewhere there was a set of books that would appeal to children and endow teachers with the magic that would enable them to survive the weekly Lord's Day session. During the decade preceding the decline, the Seabury Series had met the major educational needs of the church. The only evidence of this once-vigorous endeavor were stacks of expensive and dust-gathering books and the nagging suspicion that the Seabury "method" had ceased to be a viable approach for the local congregation.

Planned and built in the expansive optimism of the late 1950s, the educational building, with its thirty-nine rooms, was identified as a negative asset. The fourteen-by-twenty-three-foot rooms were prototypes of the ordered and familiar sterility of the public school. This ecclesiastical adaptation was outfitted with closely graded furniture, colored chalkboards, adjustable storage, and child-height plumbing. Everything was modern, clinical, and frightfully dull. The feel of the place was essentially that of the institutions in which the youngsters spent their five-day weeks. Erected at immense expense, the building and its furnishings were evidence that the church had, unwittingly perhaps, espoused the belief that learning was possible and would only take place within the boundaries of the model dictated by the more professional world of public education. The presence of books, bells, chalk, and teachers were solemn reminders to the children that Sunday was another day on which one attended school. Sunday school was indeed a "school," but one forced to operate without the social and legal sanctions supporting compulsory education. The conviction emerged that St. Luke's Sunday school was just too *much* of a school and that by its name and structure it was communicating the negative authoritarian dimensions that were by now even eroding the effectiveness of secular education.

In tandem with the dissatisfaction over curriculum and the

rigidities of the physical plant, there was the change in the personality and outlook of the typical Sunday school pupil. It is an acknowledged fact that the children of the seventies are profoundly conditioned by electronic media. Their learnings are increasingly visual and, as a result of "studying" at the television set, they are members of a generation that has escaped from the control and limitations of the printed text. Technology has produced a range of experiences and realities not found in nature or in traditional sociological forms. The growing inattentiveness and discipline problems attaching themselves to the usual Sunday school setting appeared to be symptomatic of young persons who had been satiated by a diet more varied than that the church was offering. If these children were to hear the Good News, a more sophisticated and comprehensive educational vehicle was indicated.

In its search for a viable Sunday morning in Christian training, St. Luke's was aided by the insights of two people. The disparate geniuses of Dr. Ronald Goldman of England and Mr. Walt Disney of Hollywood provided the inspiration necessary. Goldman, in his book, *Readiness for Religion,*[1] had proposed teaching of religion by use of "the real life experiences of . . . children." These so-called "life-themes" can be developed upon "any area of a child's life, of which he has firsthand knowledge." In the opinion of Margaret E. Hughes, who has applied Goldman's theory in curriculum development, a life-theme is "where we begin with the real-life experience of children, and through this lead them to see its religious significance."[2] In its initial emphasis the approach is unapologetically secular. That to which children have already been exposed, the immediate and concrete experiences that make up their world, is the medium by which they move toward religious insights and learnings. The use of life themes requires a lively faith in the validity and universality of "incarnation." The teacher must, with the Psalmist, be convinced that the heavens and all of creation are "telling the glory of God." If life in its totality is a

1. Ronald Goldman, *Readiness for Religion: A Basis for Developmental Religious Education* (New York: Seabury Press, 1970).

2. Margaret E. Hughes, *The Importance of Bread* (New York: Morehouse-Barlow, 1970).

sacramental witness to the presence and activity of the Creator, then the familiar tokens of bread, water, light, sheep, fish, and human relationships can become the stuff for the nurturing of believers. The theological assumption is that through the participation in and the penetration of a life-theme the student is confronted with the divine reality that infuses all of existence. In Goldman's approach, religion is not relegated to a special area of experience or revelation. Life-theme teaching emphasizes the "interrelatedness of all knowledge." The motivation of the learner is also a positive factor. The life-theme is an area of explorable data in which there is already an existing "natural interest."

The Goldman methodology had, apparently, been framed with the typical classroom in mind. However, after accepting the validity and potential in life-theme teaching, the people at St. Luke's Church sensed that the right-angled rigidities of the classroom were at cross-purposes with approach. Sunday schools, as mentioned earlier, are in trouble in part because they have the look and feel of the familiar and often-despised classroom. The environment itself communicates and it communicates ofttimes more vividly than the words uttered within it. If a teacher had chosen water for a life-theme, the ideal place for its exploration would be the seashore, lakeside, or stream bank. But, as the classroom cannot always be readily transported to the primary environment, the next best would be to so design the teaching situation as to approximate it. At St. Luke's Church the conflict between a life-theme and an incongruent milieu was resolved by the work of the late master of fantasy, Mr. Walt Disney. In the building of his "Magic Kingdom" the filmmaker revolutionized the entertainment industry. A product of Hollywood, Disney designed his theme parks on the model of the motion picture set. Disneyland and Disneyworld are, beneath the surface, ever-changing sets open to the public. Traveling through its several spaces, one becomes an "actor." The environment, by its simulated and comprehensive reality, invites participation. A marriage of Goldman and Disney resulted in the fabrication of life-theme environments for the communication of the Good News.

A "tour" through a church-based environment called "Mill

Street," used in the winter of 1974, will illustrate the thematically controlled approach to Christian education. The life-theme was "bread" and the initial input was from the printed curriculum, *The Importance of Bread.* A planning committee, composed of lay persons and a parish priest, addressed itself to the type of learnings, activities, and materials that were to be used in the several subsections of the environment. Working within the possibilities and limitations imposed by the space available, five groupings of learning were fixed upon. Within "Mill Street" there would be an eating facility, a biblical heritage area, a craft room, a laboratory in which to explore scientific understandings, and a fun zone. In each of the sections the primary focus would be upon bread, but in each the life-theme would be approached from a unique perspective. The learning-activity designs were planned to be completed in a ten to fifteen minute period. The students, participating in each of the areas on a rotational basis, would in the course of the session be exposed to a multifaceted experience.

Pupil circulation through the five areas of "Mill Street" and regular attendance was encouraged by an extension of the environment into their homes. Prior to the opening of the school, each parish youngster in grades one through six received through the mails a book of predated "Mill Street Super Coupons." On the Sunday indicated on the face of the coupon the child would be admitted to the wonders of "Mill Street." On the reverse side of the ticket was a form for the name and address of the bearer. Collected and logged by the gatekeeper it served as an accurate attendance record for the school. Included in each coupon book were several "visitor's passes," valid on any Sunday. These served to encourage new members to join the program. When relinquished at the gate the ticketholders were given a plastic envelope containing five paper coins. The name and the logo of each of the sections on the street were printed on the coins. Spending the coins, the student moved through the several areas, participating in the activities inside.

The "set" designed to contain the bread unit was a turn-of-the-century rural American village. Heavy with nostalgia, the theme-environment lent credence to an understanding of the growing of wheat, its uses and meaning in society and church. Entering "Mill Street" the participant encountered first "Grandmother's Kitchen," the eating facility. Behind the painted Victorian exterior was an inviting old-fashioned kitchen. Cast-iron pots hung on papered walls. Dishes were in the Welsh cupboard. A wood-burning range (minus the fire) was centered at the back of the room. At the center was a rectangular table, gingham covered and set for twelve with a glass-shaded lamp suspended over it. Presiding at the table was a "grandmother" from the parish membership. On the mailbox, mounted outside of the room, her name was stenciled. The coordinator, who was present but in the background, prepared a variety of breads with a different one for each Sunday in the unit. At each setting there was placed a card upon which was printed a classic table grace and as the grandmother served the bread the prayer was said by the group. During the course of the meal grandmother would interact with the youngsters, sharing informally with them anecdotes from her home and childhood and perhaps photographs from long ago. The children proved attentive, the atmosphere relaxed, and the setting had about it a eucharistic dimension.

Next door to "Grandmother's Kitchen" was the Biblical heritage area, "The Nickelodeon." The walls, covered with colored butcher paper, were painted to resemble an early theater. A carved and antiqued piano contributed to the music-hall feeling. Erected at the far end of the room was a false wall decorated in reds, purples, and gold, to simulate a stage. A rectangular opening in the wall was draped with curtains. The "stage" was used for story dramatizations with hand-held puppets. Covered by a movie screen or flannel board, the same area was adapted to projected or cutout visuals. The activities in "The Nickelodeon" were strictly religious in nature. During the twelve weeks of "Mill Street," the great "bread" stories from the Old and New Testaments were communicated with the help of the supportive environment.

The craft area was known as the "Red Barn." A false-front, board-and-batten "barn" had been built and covered the glass entry. Inside, the room was converted to simulate the interior of a barn, and farm implements were integrated into the decor. A plank table was supported by sawhorses, and bales of straw provided the seating. The craft projects were dictated by the bread life-theme. Dough was formed and sculptured. Samplers were made incorporating the petition "give us this day our daily bread." Small breadboard plaques were assembled, and lacquered to their face was a tested whole wheat bread recipe and the words, "I am the bread that came down from heaven." Lathe and cardboard shadow boxes were made and in each a single stalk of wheat was glued.

In the "Old Mill" the scientific dimensions of the life-theme were explored. A water-driven grist mill was painted on the exterior of the room and the illusion carried through to the interior. Fabric flour sacks, filled with pillow stuffing, were piled along one wall. A millstone, on loan from a milling company, added an authentic note. Small loaf pans were filled with grains and appropriately labeled. Soils were analyzed for their growing properties. Seeds were sprouted and the resulting vegetation tasted. Wheat was ground into flour and on two occasions quick-rising breads were baked and eaten. The mysterious property of yeast and its function in bread making was investigated.

"Country Carnival," the fifth area, was devoted to what its name implied—a fun zone. Suspended from the ceiling was a tentlike canopy. A selection of rustic, home-fabricated games stood around the perimeter of the room. Participants were invited to try their luck, and scores were recorded on individual cards prepared for the purpose. Small prizes were awarded and everyone was a winner. "Country Carnival" was also the headquarters for the "Mill Street Memory Verse" competition. In the mail each week during the program, pupils received a card on which a Bible verse relating to the life-theme was printed. On the reverse there was space for a parent's signature, indicating that the student had memorized and satisfactorily recited the reference. When presented to the section coordinator, the contestant was invited to choose a special gift from the "Treasure Chest," an ancient steamer trunk salvaged and colorfully decorated.

Into each of the thematically developed units there had been integrated a service or missionary project. The projects selected were related, as far as possible, to the life-theme under consideration. During the weeks of "Mill Street," small wooden barrels, appropriately labeled, were distributed, in which to collect coins to be used to purchase bread for our friends in Navajoland. The unit on "air" directed funds to the CROP agency with the provision they be used for the purchasing of windmills destined for underdeveloped areas. "Genesisland," an out-of-doors summer program, with its emphasis on green and living things, studied and gave to the Heifer Project.

Frequent mailings are a lively element in St. Luke's Sunday school. Children who, as a rule, receive little via the mails, find periodic arrivals a welcome experience. An individually addressed letter or package enhances self-esteem and can become an expression of the church's concern for persons as individuals. Interest in the units has been stimulated with correspondence printed on artwork letterheads designed for the purpose. Novelty mailers, a more elaborate modification of the letter, have generated interest in the programs. "Mill Street" was announced with a presession mailing of a small sack of wheat packaged with appropriate data. The "water" unit was promoted by a fossilized shark's tooth, which was incorporated into a box especially designed for it. "Genesisland," with it's walk-aboard "Ark" and "Adam and Eve's Garden," was introduced by a mailer whose cover asked the question: "When the Ark hit land, what did Mr. Noah do?" Inside a packet of mixed vegetable seeds and the injunction to "plant seeds", as did the primeval sailor who turned to farming once the waters had receded. Though requiring hours of cutting and pasting, the effort is well worth it as the mailings extend the teaching environment into the homes of the students.

Leadership in the thematically developed units has been administered by a team of coordinators who oversee the several learning areas. While present each Sunday, the coordinator is not necessarily the teacher for the session. Volunteers, some engaged for a single period, are encouraged to participate. The life-theme method, with its frankly secular trappings, has motivated many adults, who formerly had declined the invitation to help in Sunday School—explaining that they "know nothing about the Bible." When asked to share their special interest or skills, recruiting adequate leadership ceased to be a problem. Life-theme teaching also lends itself to the use of "specialists" from beyond the parish membership. On a Sunday in the "water" unit, the local navy shipyard sent two divers, who visited the school and demonstrated their deep-sea regalia. One summer "Genesisland" was visited by a trainer from a wild-animal park, who brought a lion cub. Beekeepers, wood-carvers, reptile handlers, airplane pilots, a farrier with his hammers and forge are others who contributed to the richness of the units.

Use of audio and visual media has been a part of the thematically developed environments. A room planned and decorated to resemble the living quarters of a seacoast lighthouse achieved credibility by a tape recording of crashing surf, the cry of gulls, and the moan of a distant foghorn. In the unit on "sheep and shepherds," a Bedouin-style tent was erected in a learning section. An oriental rug covered the floor and large pillows provided comfortable seating. Imagination was stimulated and storytelling enhanced by the background sounds of desert animals coming from an out-of-sight cassette player. A unit on "light" made vivid use of a series of prerecorded, custom-made "mood" tapes. The room, designed as pure science fiction, was dubbed the "Time Machine." A false wall was pierced by flashing lights and headphone consoles. Seated at the computerlike wall, the students donned their headsets and heard the space hostess issuing instructions in preparation for their journey back into time. The clanging of metallic doors, the roar of rocket engines, and the pulse of radio signals provided atmosphere for the recorded story that would follow when the time-travelers had reached their destination. In the first thematically structured unit, one dealing with fish, an "undersea" voyager came to life through the use of a media mix. A small enclosed room was built within an existing classroom and entry was by a crawl-through tunnel. Behind openings in the room-within-a-room, lighted fish tanks containing living specimens were placed. Another opening was covered by a rear-projection screen upon which were shown a series of single-concept, Super Eight films on sea life. With the playing of a tape of undersea sounds, the visitors were transported into an almost-believable world.

"The Great American Dirigible and Lighter than Air Craft Co., Ltd." and the eight other thematically designed environments have afforded a frame within which the Good News has been proclaimed to the children at St. Luke's Church. Pedagogically, the program may be open to criticism. But those involved, however, have not had the time to worry about that: once delivered from the burden of a traditional Sunday school, the participants in this home-grown venture have been having just too much fun! With the likes of Dr. Goldman and Mr. Disney, the blessing of hammers and nails, the potential of tapes and films, the assistance of the United States Post Office, the discovery of a fossil supply store in Fort Worth, lay people who are free to dream, and children whose enthusiasm never runs thin—the Lord's Day has become a very exciting day in the week.

·6·

People as Content: Adult Christian Education as Evoking and Interpreting the Stories of People

RICHARD W. GILLETT

The minister is on the phone. He has a need: to find a chairperson for the parish supper that precedes the parish annual meeting. The date is coming up fast, and he is close to panic after having three persons turn him down. He finally thinks of Jane, a new parishioner. He calls her. "Hello, Jane? This is Roger Richards at the church. Listen, I have this need . . ." (he explains).

To the minister's vast relief, Jane says yes. His request has stirred a memory within her of her childhood decades ago in Appalachia. She begins to tell Roger Richards of her mother's suppers at the church in the small mining town where they lived. "Mother and other women in our community cooked dinner every Friday night for the striking coal miners and their families. I've always remembered their staring, sunken eyes and the sad faces of their children. . . ."

"How interesting. Well listen, Jane, about this dinner: I expect about a hundred and fifty people. . . ."

Thus passes unperceived a golden moment. It is a moment rich in potential for the Christian Education ministry of Roger's church; a moment unrecognized, certainly, because of the minister's urgent (and legitimate) need for a parishioner to fill a slot. But a moment also unrecognized because the minister—and by implication many of us who work in that field called Christian Education—is not equipped to see the richness of people's personal stories as the very stuff and content of Christian Education.

We have indeed made some strides in recent years in appreciating that a teacher-pupil "learning-the-facts" mode of Christian Education is an inadequate and not very creative approach. There is increasing appreciation that the learning process, especially in a Christian community, is much broader than this. But there is still that strong temptation to look at adults in our parishes either as receivers of our teaching (even if refined from the days of catechetical indoctrination); as people whose talents we need to tap (say, for parish suppers or for church school teaching); as able administrators or decision makers (vestry); or as handy men or women who can help hold the church fabric together.

The thoughts I share in these few pages come from a mere handful of moving experiences I've had when I've taken the time to listen a bit to peoples' stories of their lives and those of their predecessors. I've also reflected upon the reasons for the popularity of the book and TV program "Roots" in our time. And I have begun to understand that there are hidden episodes in the journeys of us all that may be strikingly parallel at times to the Great Journey of the people of God through the Old and New Testaments—and, therefore, susceptible of being endowed with transforming religious power.

I hasten to say that I offer here no model of a successful parish program based upon these ideas (anyway I suspect that many of the stories of successful programs written up in the various church journals might not be quite that successful or replicable!); only some perceptions and some ideas, which are largely untried.

But it also should be said that if these perceptions have validity, the oft-heard complaint by small or financially struggling parishes that they haven't the resources to develop a good Adult Education program is hereby disarmed. For all parishes have people! All people have histories. And all parishes are situated in communities where people of surprisingly diverse histories and backgrounds live, comprising communities that themselves have histories.

The importance of getting people to tell their stories—of "people as content"—needs to be seen in the context of the times in which we live. And to live at the end of an era, as we do, is an unsettling experience. It is the end of an era that began over two centuries ago with the Industrial Revolution. Along with that end, we are seeing the end of the global domination of thought modes, culture, and policies that originated with the West (that is, the culture in which we live). What new era is in the offing we do not know. But the effect upon the endeavor of Christian Education of living in an "Age of Uncertainty" (to use the title of the popular TV series by John Kenneth Galbraith), versus what it was like to carry on that endeavor in an age of greater certainty, is profound and is worth briefly considering here.

In an age of greater certainty, such as seemed to prevail in America until the unsettling questions of the 1960s pushed themselves to the forefront, the rightness of one's past heritage was seldom questioned. "Western civilization" has been for us the carrier of all the essential human values, along with our Christian heritage, and the two were more often than not seen as coterminous. In other words, when you are sure of your past, you do not look at it or think about it very much. The epitome of this sense of certainty about one's past, and a resultant disdain of it, is Henry Ford's remark in the confident post-World War I era that "history is bunk."

But in times of social and cultural uncertainty such as our own, the compass needle of security swings wildly and erratically to and fro. And when the present thus frightens or unnerves us, we are moved to look into the past for symbols, moods, and moments of security, which we seem unable to find in the present. What are we looking for? Well, stripped of all intellectualizing, perhaps it's a bare-bones evidence of how our ancestors, or other individuals or groups in the past, encountered uncertainty and adversity and lived through it—occasionally even triumphing over it. Hence the almost faddish proportions of genealogical research today, and the popularization of "Roots" on many levels, can be seen as including precisely such motives.

In our churches, we have not been totally unmindful of the importance of the past. In confirmation classes and in other courses, we have sought (for example) to describe our Anglican heritage and to uncover for people the reasonableness of the "via media." But the teaching of our heritage only as "history"—even as *church* history—suffers from a crucial defect: namely that our church history is predominantly western-based. And it is precisely the observation that many of the great Western ideas and thought modes that we absorbed as children are *not* making headway but are rather becoming obsolescent in their application to world problems that creates a sense of uneasiness about looking at the past in the way we in the churches (or outside of them) have traditionally done.

Here is where a look at the phenomenal popularity of "Roots" can enlighten us. How do you explain its popularity? Of course, the story itself is one of immense drama, suspense, and human heroism. And it is connected to our collective past as Americans in an unmistakable way.

But "Roots" was not merely a story, it was a *pilgrimage*. It told of conflict, suffering, endurance, and triumph. And the *way in which it was told*—as the story of Alex Haley, a real-life black descended from the slave Kunta Kinte, who was likewise real—was crucial to its success. For it was *not* a history of slavery's history in Africa and the American south. No, it was one of our contemporaries telling his story to us. And the telling of that story in such personal terms (for all the negatives of its subsequent ballyhooing) filled our present with more significance and made our future together (as blacks and whites) more hopeful.

Such personal biographical stories have the power to break through history, keeping hope alive while our understanding of where history itself may be taking us remains unclear.

Given the desirability of getting people to "tell their story"—a "people as content" approach, as I would call it—what is the particularly religious dimension of this approach? What might some examples be? How would one proceed to make it happen in a parish or community? Finally, would the result of all this be a measurable advancement of the Christian Gospel?

First, it may be helpful to say what "the religious dimension" to telling one's story does *not* mean. It does not mean primarily telling our stories of belonging to such-and-such a church, or how good or bad our Sunday School was when we were children. It may include such accounts; but the central story we all have to tell is one of a life lived in the world. It is with imparting religious significance the totality of that life lived in the world that we are concerned.

Nor do we mean by telling one's story a psychological self-analysis of why one's personality turned out the way it did. The unhappy (or happy!) childhood syndrome, complete with description of dominating fathers and overworked, neurotic mothers, is not the focus.

A most helpful book, *Biography as Theology*, by James William McClendon, Jr. (Abingdon Press paperback, 1974), addresses itself to our questions. Theology is in a shift in our times, says McClendon, a Professor of Theology at Church Divinity School of the Pacific. The shift is pervasive and a new approach is needed. McClendon proposes an approach he calls the "ethics of character-in-community" (admitting at once the awkwardness of the phrase). To explain his approach, he examines the lives of four persons: Dag Hammarskjöld, secretary-general of the United Nations; Martin Luther King, Jr.; Clarence Jordan of Koinonia Farms, Georgia; and, interestingly, the American composer Charles Edward Ives. Probing their significance, he finds that their lives exhibit what he calls an "ethics of character"; and indicates that underlying this, if one probes with the eyes of faith, there is to be found a theology of character.

To some readers, it might sound a bit like playing around with words. One difficulty may be that the word "character," as applied to a people-as-content approach, conjures up some nineteenth-century Victorian moral-betterment images, which went out of favor with our grandparents! But the terminology does not matter much if the thesis is relevant. And McClendon's thesis is that "By recognizing that Christian beliefs are not so many propositions to be catalogued or juggled like truth-functions in a computer, but are living convictions which give shape to actual lives and actual communities, we open ourselves to the possibility that the only relevant critical examination of Christian beliefs may be one which begins by attending to lived lives. Theology must be at least biography."

But if theology must be at least biography, can biography always become theology? That would seem to be a relevant question. For if we are to look at "people as content," how do we begin to theologize about our lives?

McClendon, in his chapter on Martin Luther King, remids us of the power that the Bible had in the civil-rights movement. King gave prominence and power to the black insight that the Old Testament story of the Exodus out of bondage from Egypt was intimately connected with the interpretation blacks made of their experience in America. King saw the situation the American black was in. And, says McClendon, he applied the images of Exodus: oppressive Pharoahs, Hebrews longing for freedom from Egypt, the threatening wilderness, and the Promised Land. King's own story became, in this historic instance, the story of his own people.

Thus, an "ethics of character"—the actual behavior of King through his own nonviolent direct action, beginning with the Montgomery bus boycott—became a *theology* of character when the biblical metaphors were appropriated into the experience. They thus gave transforming religious power not only to an individual (King) but to an entire people.

For Dag Hammarskjöld, another of McClendon's biographical sketches, the case was different. Hammarskjöld belonged to no church, nor was he the leader of a movement. But his remarkable diary, *Markings,* shows us that in addition to his explicit, frequent use of the Bible, he was interpreting his life through the use of biblical metaphors: servant, cross, journey, frontier.

Summing up his own thoughts, McClendon asserts that one way in which we theologians, priests, or teachers may do better work is through attention to compelling biographies. And a key to unlocking these biographies is to be found in the dominant or controlling images that may be found in the lives of which they speak. (For King, the Egyptian bondage, the exodus, the Promised Land; for Hammarskjöld, the servant, the "One," brother.)

I would like to press McClendon's thought further: Why limit our attention to compelling biographies, i.e., the interpretation of famous and well-known lives? As will be gathered from the opening incident of this article (an incident only partly fictitious), our parishioner Jane had a story in her "biography" that her minister missed. For even in that brief snapshot of her life and her mother's life back in Appalachia, in which hungry miners and their children were fed, she transmitted an episode filled with potential biblical images! The feeding of the five thousand, the provision of manna in the wilderness, the Messianic banquet parable of Jesus in which those from the highways and byways are fed, all are there. And who knows what others would turn up if Jane's life and her mother's, together with their interaction with the community, had been further explored?

This, then, is to assert that, if we look for them even in the most ordinary of people, there are present—if they are encouraged to tell their stories and those of their forebears—the themes of the Sacred Story. That is, does everybody have somewhere in his or her past an Abrahamic journey, an exodus, a time of wandering in the wilderness, a promised land, an exile, a crucifixion, a resurrection, or a new fire? My urging would be that, in faith, we proceed boldly on that assumption. And that by doing so, a number of benefits will accrue. One, we will enhance the value in our parishes of persons in and of themselves and not just in what they can do for the church. Two, in this reflection upon the meaning of our and others' past, a surer tie will be established with pasts that have much to teach us and much with which to ennoble us. Three, that in attempting to understand application of biblical themes and images, we all just might learn a little bit more about the relevance of the Bible. And four (perhaps it is obvious), that we will discover that you cannot encourage people to tell their stories and those of their forebears without hearing also the stories of the communities in which they lived. Indeed, it is in the interaction of people with their communities that precisely the richest and most significant experiences are found.

It is here necessary to reflect upon the current context of our own community—both secular and religious, both local and world—as the setting in which such storytelling will take place. I would like to illustrate that context by telling you, the reader, a true story I was involved in. Indeed, it is that story that became the genesis of the thoughts and conclusions expressed in this article. It may also illustrate in a general way the power telling one's story can have.

The story started over a year ago in my front yard, where I labored one morning over a large fallen tree with a cumbersome rented chain saw. I was having a terrible time. It was several minutes before I noticed that a man and his two small boys had been watching me. The man, in his 50s, spoke to me in Spanish (I believe he'd observed the friendliness of my oldest son, a bilingual teen-ager, and surmised that I spoke Spanish also): "Do you want some help?" To my strong affirmative answer he responded, and for two hours expertly wielded the chain saw. While we (mostly he) worked, we talked in snatches, his sunburnt Aztec face and willing manner telling me something about him, along with what he said. He had come to Pasadena (my home) the year before from the province of Jalisco in Mexico, bringing six of his nine children. There, things had been desperate. "Many families are leaving. Inflation is rampant, agriculture is mechanizing, unemployment is high."

What was he doing now? He was a mostly unemployed carpenter/gardener, having skills but no stock of tools. He and his children lived two blocks away in a tiny apartment, its walls defaced by the graffiti of a neighborhood gang. His wife had died in Mexico shortly before the family decided to move north. His oldest daughter, twenty, was now the mother and head of household for the father and the other five children. She worked in a nursing home at a minimum wage.

At the end of two hours the tree had been converted to firewood. To my offer of payment, he simply replied, "No es nada." It is nothing; a man helps his neighbor wherever he may be.

Some months passed, and Christmas was upon us. I remembered the family, and two of my children and I went to visit. I decided that, in addition to the gesture of some Christmas money (a feeble gesture compared to the natural kindness of a man who'd helped his neighbor with a tree), I could check with the Department of Public Social Services to see if the family was eligible for any form of public assistance. His daughter and I went to the office. The answer, polite but firm, was that being "illegal aliens" they were eligible for nothing. The daughter's reaction was bravely cheerful: "We lost nothing by asking."

That night I visited their house. Miguel (not his real name) offered me a beer, while the little kids bounced around the living room. We talked a little more. It was small talk—friendly, inconsequential. A friend of his son's joined us, and more beer was opened. The hospitality of a Mexican man and his children was simply continuing, no more, no less.

And that is the story. It is a simple story, etched with courage and cheer as well as tragedy and sadness. It could well end there without further pondering—a moving account of real human lives. But a reflection upon the story—specifically that Miguel and his family were who they were—inextricably draws in Miguel's own origin, roots, and Mexican community as part of it; draws in ultimately, in fact, such abstract considerations as Mexican-American relations, and thereby the larger justice issues shaking a world so sharply demarcated between rich and poor. (Even as we'd talked, down in Mexico the peasants were marching in their desperation, while here in the United States stricter regulations had just been placed upon "illegal aliens" like Miguel and his family, deporting them to Mexico in greater numbers.)

It is therefore essential that, whenever such storytelling can be evoked, we attempt to engage in that process not only our own parishioners but those in the community who may have backgrounds different from our own; backgrounds that, if better understood, can begin to build some bridges across the chasms of suspicion, fear, and ignorance, which tragically separate race from race and class from class.

And what of the biblical images and metaphors we are supposed to look for in such stories? In this one of Miguel and his family, the biblical images leaped out: Abraham, looking for the promised land; the exiles in Babylon; Joseph and Mary, looking for room at the inn. And a parable told by Jesus: "Lord, when was it that we saw you hungry and fed you, or thirsty and gave you drink?" And our Lord answers the righteous: "Inasmuch as you have done it to one of the least of these my brothers and sisters, you have done it to me.

In fact, the thought later came to me with a jolt: Miguel had said he was a carpenter.

How might one begin to make such storytelling happen both in a parish and in a community? I confess I do not know; the idea is too new with me. Small group discussion seems an obvious way to begin. One-on-one interviews would seem so, too. But it should be obvious also that one's story cannot be forced; the climate must be propitious, the soil right.

The essential ingredients of such storytelling I feel rather certain of, however: that interpretation of one's story against the backdrop of her/his community in present and past be made; that we must proceed on the assumption that everyone—both the recognized and the unrecognized in society—has a story; and that there are biblical paradigms, symbols, and themes waiting to be applied to all our stories, to enrich them, and to transform both the listeners and the tellers with liberating religious power. That is Christian education!

And such liberating religious power, by definition, will be unable to keep to itself, but will break out into actions that humanize all of us, humanize the community, and bring closer together that entire people whom God, beginning with Abraham, is calling us all to be.

·7·

CITY'S GARDEN

ELYSE BRADT

One of the jobs of a Christian educator is to gather, interpret, and transfer the rich fertile images of the Bible and church history to that which is rich, creative, and productive in our lives today. This chapter tries to demonstrate how this can happen in a small urban mission.

Three elements are used in our approach to developing a curriculum: study (knowledge), prayer (unity), and work (action).

Study looks at questions like "What is the story the Bible is telling?" "What is our history saying to us?" "Why did the Church move in this particular way?"

Prayer looks at worship and explores the ways that prayer keeps us together (unity).

Work takes the knowledge handed down and interpreted from the Bible and church history and the unifying force of prayer and worship and develops a way to use both those elements in everyday living. This element is the window-box garden of the city. This is where faith takes root, sprouts and flourishes.

The examples in this chapter of study and prayer are much more universal in their usefulness for black and non-black churches because the historical roots of Christianity and the history of blacks and whites in this country are part of the same history. The worship and prayer-lives of both blacks and nonblacks reflect concerns of a common heritage.

Work, on the other hand, is a product of the immediate social order, i.e., the neighborhood and the economic environment surrounding the church building.

Since blacks in America cross all economic, social, and educational lines, it is impossible to expect that this chapter will reflect the *black social order*—there is none. What this chapter does provide is an example of how one urban church used its history, its prayer, and its worship to develop a curriculum for social change and awareness. I hope some of its insights, knowledge, faith and creativity will be useful to other churches.

STUDY

If we are to bridge the gap between the Bible and our lives today, we need to first explore our own experiences in light of the Scriptures.

The history of the Israelite people as recorded in the Old Testament is not the unique experience of one people in one place at one time. The faith of Abraham and the zeal of the prophets for justice are repeated at different times by different peoples throughout the world. The story of balck men responding to God's call in naked faith and proclaiming his justice to a selfish and indifferent people is sacred history too. Through it, God acts again in history to reveal himself to us, to recreate us and to establish his rule.

What is the mission of a people on earth in relation to the Eternal? How can a people find meaning in the suffering that they as a group have endured? How can they deal with people whose lives and purposes are evil? How can they themselves avoid believing that the evil of their neighbors is actually right and good?

The ancient Israelites faced these questions and others like them throughout their history. Although we have not always articulated them, we have faced and are still facing these questions, too. We need to examine our history to see clearly both how our ancestors have confronted and answered them and the historical situations that helped determine the answers they gave. We need to explore the possible responses in our time, not only in terms of our present situation, but also in the light of the Scripture. This chapter will give you a sample of just how our churches began to do that.

Sample of Reading for a Unit on Faith

The following are highlights from a study used in our churches that illustrate the kind of basic reading that Church School teachers would do and from this draw activities and discussions for children or adult classes.

Faith has been the basis of life for black people in America for the last three hundred years. Although we shall single out this subject for discussion in the first section, in an important sense a faith history, such as we are dealing with here, must necessarily be about faith from beginning to end. Our confrontation with evil and injustice and our attempts to build community, for example, are as much expressions of our faith as our endurance and courage during slavery. Indeed, as we shall discover in this first section, faith for black people in America has taken many different forms and has been expressed in many different modes.

For the black American, faith has seldom been simply an intellectual assent to a body of principles and beliefs. For the black American, faith has been a way of looking at life and dealing with life situations in the light of belief. Based on a belief in a God who wills that all men should live in a world where justice, peace, love and total well-being prevail, and on the certainty that God can work through men to bring into being the kind of world he desires, the faith of the Afro-American has been expressed as much in heroic endurance as in dramatic action.

In the life of Frederick Douglass, for example, the great risks incurred in his escape from slavery and work for the abolition of that evil institution seem typical of the actions of a man of faith. Faith, after all, does imply a certain willingness to risk security and loss as one ventures into the unknown. The response of a man like Douglass may characterize faith for the man who has been caught up in God's vision and has the opportunity, imagination, and courage to pursue it; however, for the man who has seen the vision but who is prevented from pursuing it—the slave in Mississippi, for example, for whom all thought of escape or rebellion was unrealistic—the faith response must be quite different. For the man whose vision is constantly frustrated, faith may be expressed in prophetic and apocalyptic proclamations, descriptions of heaven, or simply heroics. To meet and face frustration every day with confident endurance is one such act of heroism. To believe that the Lord of the past will provide as well in the future also involves a willingness to risk. It involves a willingness to risk cynicism, despair, madness, and the urge to suicide as one constantly reaffirms in his attitude toward life the vision of a world that seems destined never to become a reality.

That was the faith of slave rebels and the black abolitionists, educators, and civil rights leaders—the faith of our martyrs, as well. Now, just as then, as we view the crumbling neighborhoods where the masses of our people live, as we face teachers and employers who are convinced that we are less able than others solely because we are black, faith is the most important ingredient in our struggle for freedom and the right to live creative and meaningful lives as free people.

Slavery

(Teachers are asked to read this as background for later discussions.)

The situation of a slave in the United States was far different from that of the slaves in ancient civilizations and in Africa. Chief Justice Roger B. Taney's opinion in the Dred Scott Case (1857) that "Negroes . . . are so far inferior that they have no rights which the white man is bound to respect" only made explicit what had been taken from granted ever since slavery had become a going concern in this country.[1] Of course, Justice Taney's opinion was wrong in the light of Christian doctrine. Since God is the Father of all men, no people is inherently inferior to any other. All men are brothers and equal under God. But Taney's position was necessary for the efficient operation of the slave system in this country.

Many scholars believe that the type of slavery practiced in the United States was particularly likely to be psychologically crippling for the slave because meaningful contacts between slave and free society were minimized.

One of the most important legacies of slavery is the effect of a period of servitude on the personality of the ex-slaves. They show marked evidence of regression to infantile behavior. Some Jewish authorities argue that Moses purposely kept his people in the wilderness until all who had been slaves would not have the courage to fight their way into Canaan.[2]

---

1. *Quarrels That Have Shaped the Constitution,* Garraty, John A., ed. (New York: Harper and Row, 1964), p. 86.
2. Deborah Pessin, *Jewish People* (New York: United Synagogue Book Service, 1951-1953).

In their degradation, the slaves in the United States turned frequently to religion and especially to the biblical account of the Israelites in bondage in Egypt. Their common legacy to future generations of blacks in America was the spirituals they wove from these biblical stories. Of course, many of the spirituals served as a code to notify or warn those who were waiting for an opportunity to escape to the free states in the North. But for those who could find no means of escape and for those who could not even entertain such thoughts, their religion, the spirituals, and the Bible held out hope in a time of darkness. For the slaves remembered that God had forced Pharoah to free the Israelite slaves and strongly believe that he would move in some way to free them, also.

SESSION I

Objective: To review and discuss the material on faith.

As a means of opening discussion on the section on faith, you may want to focus on an issue such as, "I want to have faith in the potential I think God gave me, but I find it difficult when other people put me down." One way of beginning such a discussion might be to read or tell an open-ended story such as the one below. Open-ended stories are frequently used in storytelling in east Africa.

> Jennie Mae is a high-school student who had gone one day during summer vacation to do a day's work for Mrs. Jones. Mrs. Jones taught at Centerville High School and normally employed Jennie Mae's mother to clean for her on Thursdays. Because Jennie Mae's mother had some business to transact, however, she had sent Jennie Mae in her place. When it came time for lunch, Mrs. Jones began to talk to the girl about her plans for the future. Jennie Mae told the teacher that she wanted to go to college and become a hospital dietitian. Mrs. Jones asked Jennie Mae what grades she had received in school so far. Jennie Mae told her that she had very good grades in math and science, but that she had not done well in English. She explained that she wasn't interested in English and had stopped writing reports for English classes because the teachers had often harshly criticized the reports from black students in front of the class. Mrs. Jones replied that she didn't think that Jennie Mae should try to go to college. It was expensive and, since there was a lot of writing to do in college, she might flunk out. "Besides," she added, "you'll just have to come back to cook in someone's kitchen. Even if

> you do get all that training, Centerville Hospital doesn't have any Negro dietitians."
>
> As the discussion continued, Jennie Mae became more and more concerned. Mrs. Jones was known to be a teacher who had worked hard to prepare some of Centerville's best white students for Harvard and Yale. She knew a lot about what was expected in college courses. Jennie Mae suspected that Mrs. Jones had advised her not to try to go to college largely because she was black. Of course, Mrs. Jones was right about the money. College *was* expensive. Perhaps she shouldn't take all that money away from the family when she might flunk out anyway.

During the discussion you may want to compare Jennie Mae's situation to that of Abraham, Frederick Douglass, or slaves in general. In addition to discussing what they would do in the situation, have the group explore how Jennie Mae may have felt. If members of the group feel that the concern noted in the story is the full extent of Jennie Mae's feelings, try to get them to probe more deeply. Help them to see that Jennie Mae, in addition to being concerned, could feel discouraged and frightened about her plans for the future. She might also feel angry toward Mrs. Jones whom she thinks might be prejudiced.

In preparation for the next session, ask the study group members to think over incidents from their own lives in which they found it difficult to maintain faith in themselves and/or God working through them. Suggest that they attempt conversations with God concerning this subject or the subject "How I came to have faith." Others might find meditation on I Kings 18:17–24 or Mark 9:14–29 helpful. These passages give some ideas as to how faith grows.

Close the session with prayer.

SESSION II

Objective: To explore the question "How do people maintain faith in themselves and/or God working through them?" in order to discover (a) what feelings are engendered in faith-crisis situations; (b) what decisions were made in these situations; and (c) what factors contributed to bolstering faith at these times.

Since various members of the study group have come prepared to discuss with the others instances from their own lives when they have found it difficult to maintain faith in themselves and/or in God working through them, the leader can simply facilitate this process. It would be good to elicit from each person (a) his feelings in the situation; (b) what decision he made; and (c) which factors, in his opinion, helped him keep faith during this time. Some such factors might include the knowledge that other people had faith in him, previous successes in that area, or the strength of his own religious and prayer life. List these factors on the board or on newsprint and save them for later sessions.

Close the session with prayer. If the group is working on its first project, ask that they consider spending some time in meditation before the next session. Perhaps they could try putting together and using a short liturgical prayer office on faith before the next session. If the group has had previous experience in working on a project ask them to watch for any categories of people (for example, high school graduates or dropouts who are job or college applicants, etc.) in the parish or community who will especially need faith in whatever they are trying to do and, in all probability, will have little support in maintaining that faith.

SESSION III

Objective: To explore the decision-making process so that the group is able to make decisions involving the proposed project that take into account all the possible alternatives, weigh the cost of any solution versus its promise, etc.

To open the session, the leader may point out that in discussing various instances during the last session in which members of the study group had personally found it difficult to maintain faith, each had told, not only how he felt in the situation and what factors enabled him to maintain faith but also what decision he made in the situation. The session included both a discussion of the feelings engendered and the decision that was made, because feelings about a situation often play an important part in determining what decision is made. Illustrate this point by using the following fictitious case history or use another case history (true or fictitious) that lends itself to this discussion, or adapt one of the incidents related by a studygroup member during the last session.

> Darryl was sixteen years old and had quit school. He had been looking for a job for three months. A friend of his told him that he

> had just got a job with the A&P and that he thought that they were still hiring. Darryl went to the local A&P where he was told to go to a downtown office. At the downtown office a receptionist gave him an application form. When he had filled it in and given it back to her, the receptionist told him to return the next morning because the man in charge of hiring had left for the day. Darryl told the receptionist that he wasn't going to put up with any more "jive" and left the office, slamming the door as he went.

Did Darryl make the right decision? Did he make a decision or did he react to what he thought was going on? What external situation did Darryl face? What were his feelings in that situation? What was likely to be the consequence of his action? What were his other alternatives, if any, and what consequences were they likely to have? What is the risk involved in each alternative, and what does it promise, i.e., what good things could come about as a result of choosing that alternative? Which alternative is likely to bring about the best results and the least regrets? How should Darryl have gone about making a decision in the situation that he faced? How did his feelings affect what he did?

To sum up, the leader may point out, if it is not already clear, that we often face situations that seem to limit us or to keep us from reaching our goal. Even within these limiting circumstances, however, we often are still able to enjoy a certain amount of freedom and control of the outcome if we stop to choose among alternatives rather than react on the basis of what we feel about the situation.

Point out that it will be important for members of the study group to examine closely both the external situations and the feelings that are likely to occur in those situations as they design a project and work to carry it out. For the next session ask the members of the study group to watch for categories of people (for example, high school graduates or drop-outs who are job or college applicants) in the parish or community who will especially need faith in whatever they are trying to do and, in all probability, will have little support in maintaining that faith.

SESSION IV

Objective: To explore the feelings of others caught in faith-crisis situations, so that members of the study group will be better able to empathize with those with whom they will be working in the project.

A chart with column headings entitled "External Situation or Problem" and "Feelings" would probably be most useful for working in this session. The leader may begin this session by getting from each person the names of categories of people who will especially need faith in whatever they are trying to do and will have little support in maintaining that faith. Have the study group choose two or three of the categories as groups they might like to design a project to work with, and put these in the right-hand column on the chart. Then elicit from the members of the study group the external situation or problem that each of the proposed groups faces and the feelings that each person involved in that situation might have. For example, suppose that one of the groups chosen is composed of students such as Jennie Mae. The external situation that these students face is the attempt, possibly prejudiced in nature, by school personnel to discourage them from trying to achieve what the students themselves feel they are capable of achieving. If the study group used Session I, they may already have outlined some of Jennie Mae's feelings in this situation (and thus the possible feelings of other students in similar circumstances). What feelings might Mrs. Jones have in the situation? What feelings might Jennie Mae's parents have? It is important to determine the range of possible feelings for all of the important people involved in the situation so as to determine what action they might take.

The leader or other study group members can suggest incidents where the members of the proposed group have to confront the external situation in which they are caught. For example, if the group has chosen teen-age boys and girls who need someone with whom they can talk out problems as a focus, the following situation can occur: Have two members of the study group act out an incident where an older boy approaches a younger one to insist that he become a member of a gang. If necessary, extend the incident to include other important persons who might not have been involved in the incident but who would be affected by the situation. Of course, after each role-play it is necessary to discuss the possible feelings of the people involved and to write these down for reference for later sessions.

For the next session ask members of the study group to think over some of the alternatives that people in the categories chosen for discussion might use to deal with the situations they face. Suggest, also, that they try Mark 9:14–29 or Psalm 123 as the basis for affective prayer, using such verses as "Lord, I believe; help thou mine unbelief" or "Have mercy upon us, O Lord, have mercy upon us" as mantras.

Close with prayer.

SESSION V

Objectives: (1) To use the decision-making process to choose goals for possible projects for each of the two or three problem situations that have been under consideration; (2) to brainstorm for objectives that would help in reaching the goal.

To make the information that will come from this session readily available, it will, perhaps, be best to make use of a chart. (See Table 7.1.)

Table 7.1 illustrates some alternatives, a goal and some possible objectives for dealing with the external situation or problem that Darryl and other job-seekers like him might face (see Session III).

Since members of the study group have come prepared to give possible alternatives for each external situation or problem under discussion, this portion of the chart can be filled in very easily. After filling in this column for each of the problem situations, have each study group member come to a decision as to which alternative for each problem he would have for a *goal.* In choosing the goal, have him carefully weigh the possible cost versus the promise of the various alternatives. Remember that one of these goals will be the goal of the project the study group will design and, thus, should offer real possibilities for helping the people who face this problem situation develop and/or maintain faith. You may want to point out, in passing, that a goal is quite often the "flip" side of a situation that we have at one time considered a problem. (Problem: I can't find a job in an environment that is not overly helpful. Goal: I'll try to find out what procedures might be involved in getting a job.)

After choosing a goal for each problem situation, the study group will *brainstorm* for *objectives* for each goal.

Up to this point in the session, in looking at the problem

Table 7.1

External Situation or Problem	Alternatives	Goals	Objectives
Trying to find a job in an environment that is not overly helpful	1) Tell off the receptionists, etc., you think might be "jiving" you. 2) Try to find out what procedures might be involved in getting a job. 3) Get training in a skill that is in demand. 4) Give up.	1) To try to find out what procedures might be involved in getting a job. 2) To carry out a course that will acquaint job-seekers with the many procedures necessary for getting a job.	1) Contact one of the job counselors at the local state employment office. 2) Develop a plan for presenting some of the usual procedures. 3) Develop a session on filling in applications. 4) Develop a session concerning interviews. 5) Get publicity and advertising out. 6) Contact people expressing interest in the course and set up dates.

situation, examining alternatives and choosing a goal, members of the study group have acted very much as though they themselves were the people involved in the problem situation. However, before brainstorming for objectives they must amend the proposed goals so that they would be suitable as the goal for the project on which they will be working (see column "Goals" on Table 7.1). Then, in formulating objectives they should feel free to consider using information, skills, etc., that may be available to members of the study group but may not be available to members of the group directly involved in the problem situation. The objectives, then, should reflect the study group's approach to attaining their goal even though the study group members have, hopefully, so identified with those involved in the situation that they keep constantly in mind the feelings, needs and desires of the other group.

Close the session with prayer. For the next session, ask the members of the study group to imagine themselves working in one of the projects outlined on the chart and consider what their feelings might be in that role. Suggest that they might also visualize themselves as one of the people actually facing the problem situation and, while imagining some specific incidents that might produce a crisis in faith, repeat one of the mantras used in prayer the week before. Some may want to continue this type of prayer over the next week.

Be sure to keep the chart developed during this session for future reference.

SESSION VI

Objective: To help each member of the study group become aware of the feelings he might possibly have as he works in the proposed project.

This is another session where a chart might be helpful. Column headings for this chart are in Table 7.2.

Table 7.2

My feelings concerning myself as participant in this project	My feelings concerning other study group members in the project	My feelings concerning people in the group facing the problem situation	My feelings concerning the people who are creating the problems

To begin this session, the leader may point out that the study group members now have some idea of the shape of the project on which they may be working. Before proceeding further, they may find it helpful to consider how they might feel working in one of these projects. Ask them to consider their feelings for each of the column headings for the above chart. In order to make the discussion more concrete, the leader might present some possible incidents that members of the study group might encounter while working on the project. For example, if working on a project with students who have been discouraged from trying to achieve their academic or career goals, study group members may encounter a great deal of hostility on the part of school personnel. How will they feel if this attitude should crop up in a meeting in which they are involved? What will their response be to that feeling? How will they feel if members of the group they are working with seem less energetic on their own behalf than the members of the study group? What if certain members of the study group seem to be doing most of the actual work? How will those who are working hardest feel about the others? How will the others feel about them? There is a wide range of possible feelings and responses under each column and for any incident. In any incident the response may be "there is no problem," "this is not my problem," "I will win," "I will be defeated." Underneath these responses there may be feelings of love, joy, anger, fear, loneliness; non-directed hostility, guilt or helplessness; misplaced self-condemnation, worthlessness or meaninglessness; or unfocused anxiety.

Where necessary, try to focus and clarify feelings as much as possible. If, for example, someone says he feels angry, ask him against whom or what he feels anger and, along with other members of the group, try to help each person focus his feelings toward appropriate targets. If someone says that some incident would make him feel worthless, have him explore with the group whether or not a feeling of worthlessness is really appropriate to that particular situation. Finally, have the group deal with their possible feelings should the project turn out to be a failure and whether, in fact, there is such a thing as failure in this project. (The project, of course, is part of a learning experience, and it seems likely that members of the study group will, necessarily, learn something that would be of use to themselves or even, eventually, in helping others, no matter what might be the outcome.)

Rather than using possible incidents drawn up by the leader (or appointed members of the group) from the outlined projects as a basis for discussion, it is possible and much more vivid to roleplay them (see Session IV). In either case, before the discussion or roleplay begins, it is essential to point out that this session is one that requires the utmost courtesy, forebearance, kindness, and love from all who participate. Obviously, each person will not respond in the same way to any given incident, and great understanding is necessary to cope with these differences in opinions and values.

For the next session ask study group members to meditate on Luke 5:18–26 and its meaning to members of the group.

Close with prayer.

SESSION VII

Objectives: (1) To facilitate acceptance of the limitations and possibilities inherent in the group project so that study group members will be freed to take effective action; (2) to choose from the projects outlined one that the group will work on.

Before members of the group discuss the Bible passage assigned at the last session in terms of its meaning for them, it is necessary to discuss it in its historical context. Either elicit from the group or point out that first-century Jews believed that sin caused physical and mental illness. Some members of the group may already have noticed (1) the extraordinary lengths to which those who carried the bed went in order to bring their friend or acquaintance to Jesus and (2) the fact that it was *their* faith and effort to which Jesus responded. Both of these facts can have great meaning for members of the study group as they begin to work with other people.

Ask if we still believe that it is possible to be paralyzed by sin. If so, in what way? Have the group look at the chart prepared in the last session and see if any of the feelings written there might tend to paralyze those in the study group as they begin work on the project. If so, what are the alternatives for dealing with them?

One obvious answer is to drop from consideration any project where there are large numbers of incapacitating feelings listed, and it might be well to stop now and choose the one project that the group will work on, if that has not already been done. Although the group's feelings concerning their involvement in the project are not the only criteria for choosing the project, they are important. Some other considerations in making a choice might include the size of the group and the extensiveness of the project or, of course, the high cost of many objectives to the people involved.

After the group has made a choice of the one project on which it will work, it is still necessary to come to grips with any counterproductive or crippling feelings that group members have listed for that project. Point out that we have already begun to deal with these feelings since we made ourselves aware of them. Ask the group how we can handle them more fully. We cannot function effectively if, for example, we feel so guilty about our own hostility that we are unable to act. Help them see that we can handle these feelings more fully by coming to accept both the limitations and the possibilities of the situation and consenting to work within them. That means accepting our own and other people's hostility, sense of helplessness and the limitations imposed by other sins and weaknesses. How is this done? By continual confession involving acceptance of what we turn away from and penance involving acknowledgment of what needs to be changed. As we accept the feelings and responses that we would turn away from and continually acknowledge the need for change, that part of those feelings and responses that could be counterproductive and incapacitate us dies. Have the group consider what possibilities are opened up for interaction within the group, or with those confronted by the problem situation, or for work within the situation itself, once these feelings have died. Help the group members to see that without these crippling feelings they will be able to have the freedom to respond to situations and to others with power, to trust and be open with each other, and to be reunited with those from whom they have been alienated. This state is part of the grace, the new and resurrected being that comes about when what has enslaved and crippled them dies by God's mercy and love, when we confess and are penitent.

Close the session with prayer. Suggest that members of the study group continue to work through their feelings in conversations with God, meditation, and effective and contemplative prayer. Suggest or have clergy or other members of the group suggest Bible passages or spiritual reading for meditation if any persons have specific problems. For example, for those who might have problems accepting the fact that some members of the study group will, in all probability, not be working as hard as others, a meditation on I Cor. 12 may be helpful. Affective prayer and contemplative prayer using Hebrews 12:1–2 may be helpful for the entire group.

SESSION VIII

Objective: To finish planning the project so that it can be put into operation.

Using that part of the chart developed in Session V, which gives the external or problem situation, alternatives, goal, and objectives for the project goal chosen in the previous session, begin this session by testing each objective against reality. Ask of each objective: "What are the positive and negative forces that would serve to enable us or hinder us in achieving this objective?" The group may find, as they weigh the answers to these questions, that some objectives will have to be modified. However, negative forces should not unduly concern the group if there are also strong positive forces present.

After testing the objectives, the group will need to set their priorities according to the time sequence in which the sessions should be conducted. For example, in the sample chart given above for Session V, contacting a job counselor at the local state employment service should precede the development of any sessions or plans for the course and, thus, is given a higher priority. Then, make a timetable for achieving the objectives.

With the help of the material from Sessions II and IV (how we develop and maintain faith; the feelings of those caught in a faith-crisis situation), brainstorm for strategies for carrying out each objective. One important strategy when working with another group is to meet with the members of that group and either secure ownership of the tentative plans that have been developed or change them to fit more closely the needs and desires of those with whom you will be working. As you develop strategies, also begin to share responsibilities and tasks and ultimate responsibility for coordinating the project; if most of the feelings concerning the project and the problem situation have been worked through, it should be relatively easy for members of the study group to assume some responsibility for executing the plan; that is, to accept the project, their roles in it, and themselves as they carry out these roles. For those who are unable to devote a lot of time to the project, there will, undoubtedly, be many small jobs, such as telephoning, which must also be done. Others may prefer to participate largely through corporate or individual prayer and thus form a supportive prayer cadre. However, it is perhaps best if those who are mainly involved through prayer be kept in touch with the active workers best for their work in the project, how the active workers feel as they work with others, how the people they work with seem to feel at various stages, etc. Whether or not all members are totally involved in the active work of the project, all can be totally involved in understanding what it is about and how it is progressing, in feeling and praying with and for those who are more actively involved, and in creatively seeking ways to support the work. The services of every person in the study group who is willing to give even a minimal amount of time to the project are valuable and can be used in some way or another.

In preparation for the next session, ask each member of the prayer group to come prepared to share with the others the prayer methods, materials, etc., that he has found most useful either in individual or group prayer during the work on the faith section. Have the group also think of materials from the black experience that could be used in the religious services that will serve as a commitment service or celebration to begin the project.

Close with prayer.

SESSION IX

Objective: To plan a religious service or celebration to begin the project.

Finish any work that has to be done to complete formulating

strategies, assigning tasks, etc. Have the group decide on a date for getting the project into full swing and a later date when the project can be evaluated and continued or evaluated and discontinued. Remind the group that the project will provide learning experiences. Ask them to jot down what they learn as they carry out the project for later discussion with the group. Ask them to note, also, any strategies that need to be revised and any unresolved feelings that might make it impossible to work effectively. Ask the study group members to try to work these feelings out individually (perhaps in the daily examination before retiring) until it is possible to work them out in the group. (Session X provides a format for such a midproject meeting.) Stress the importance of working out feelings in the group, both because several people may share the same feeling (but have been hesitant to say so) and in order to maintain the openness and trust that should have developed by this time. As members of the study group move into a more active period with the beginning of the project, suggest that they try continuing the use of prayer techniques particularly well suited to active work, such as marker prayers, short offices of prayer, conversations with God, aspirations, morning sacrifice, and evening revision. During the remainder of the session, plan the proposed religious service so that it will include those prayer techniques, materials, etc., that the members of the group have found most useful and will reflect the black faith experince.

Close with prayer.

SESSION X

Session X is optional. It can be used at any time when members of the study group who are working on the project feel a need to revise strategies or sort through unresolved feelings.

Those who have felt the need for such a session might act as leaders, relating the events or incidents that led them to assemble the group for this purpose. Each event or incident should be discussed. Although both good points and bad points should be pointed out, the thrust of the discussion should be toward discovering how things can be done better or crippling feelings can be resolved. In some cases it will be necessary to try to discover the underlying factors that have brought about the incident.

The first discussion period can be followed by a short period of silence when the group disperses. The group then reassembles to draw up some common conclusions and resolutions, although the resolutions may be made privately.

Close with spontaneous prayer.

SESSION XI

Part A

After the project has run a specified period of time, whether you wish to continue it or not it is best to have an evaluation. Some possible questions for such an evaluation are:

1. Were we able to maintain our own faith in what we were doing while working on the project? If so, how?
2. Was faith really a crucial problem for the group we chose to work with?
3. Did there seem to be an appreciable development in faith in any person(s) in the group with which you worked?
4. Was there development in any other quality (e.g., hope, love, patience)?

Part B

If the project was thought to have helped some people develop and/or maintain faith, the questions below may be useful.

1. Did the fact that other people have faith (in God, in them, in the rightness of what they were doing) help some in the group with which you were working develop or maintain faith?
2. Did the attitude of the helper (patient, concerned, kindly) seem to influence the development or maintenance of faith?
3. Did a few successful experiences seem to help some people develop or maintain faith?
4. Did you discover ways other than the ones we originally thought of that were helpful in developing and maintaining faith?
5. If it was a combination of factors that proved successful, what were the factors involved?
6. Does the project need to be continued over a longer period of time (a) in order to determine conclusively whether or not it is of use in the community; (b) because, for example, it was not publicized previously well enough for people to make use of it; (c) because it fills an important need in the community; or (d) for other reasons?

Part C

If the project did not seem to be successful, the following questions may be helpful.

1. Was the group chosen one that really needed help in developing or maintaining faith?
2. Was it so difficult for people in the two groups to relate to one another that a meaningful relationship between the two was impossible? If so, what could or what can members of the study group do to help remedy the situation?
3. Was the project unsuccessful because members of the study group lacked the necessary commitment? If so, was this because members of the study group (a) had reservations concerning the rightness or efficacy of the project; (b) were already heavily involved in other activities; (c) were not fully in agreement with the study-work-pray method; (d) were too few to carry off the project designed; or (e) for other reasons?
4. Were there other reasons that might have contributed to the failure of the project?
5. Should the project be abandoned or revamped extensively?

Be sure to allow time to discuss what members of the study group learned (about faith, about themselves, about the people they were working with, about prayer) as they worked on the project.

STEMS AND NOURISHMENT

We did a unit on faith, focusing on the faith responses of Moses and of Martin Luther King, Jr., in their individual struggles for justice for their people.

One of the resources in our neighborhood is the intergenerational family life, i.e., the extended family, with aunts, uncles, grandparents, and cousins often living in the same house. Each lesson in this unit offers an opportunity to use every age group within the family. It also gives ample opportunity for the use of games, songs, and music that the children are familiar with. Street games and movements are incorporated into a creative presentation of both the biblical story and the contemporary story.

The adults are leaders and teach the lessons in the form of a skit depicting the Bible story for the children. Then in separate classes the teen-agers act as helpers during the discussion period and work time. The children (6 to 12) are the creators, workers and producers of the final presentation of the unit; it is a uniquely intergenerational endeavor.

In this particular unit the project (action element) resulted in a slide-show presentation with accompanying skits, narration, and music for friends and neighbors.

MOSES AND MARTIN LUTHER KING, JR.—A FAITH RESPONSE

Purposes: (1) To familiarize the children with the story of Moses' and Martin Luther King Jr.'s struggle for justice, so that they can relate the stories in chronological order; (2) to help the children understand the movement of God throughout the history of a people and its leaders so that they will recognize his movement in their own lives and the lives of blacks in this country.

Lesson I: Hiding in the reeds

Pharaoh's daughter finds Moses in the reeds

Purpose: (1) To familiarize the children with the story of how Moses was found in the reeds as a baby, so that they can relate the story in their own words; (2) to help the children begin to feel the fearful atmosphere the Israelites lived with—one that caused a mother to hide her son—so that they will be able to identify situations in their own lives when they have been afraid and have had to decide what choice they had for action.

Worship

Song: "Baby Moses"

Skit/Lesson: Exodus 2:1–10, Pharoah's daughter finds Moses in the reeds.

Discussion: Can you remember why Pharaoh wanted the Hebrew children killed? When Pharaoh's daughter found Moses, whom did she choose for his nurse? How do you think the mother felt? Can you recall times when you felt afraid, so afraid that you hid away? What do you do when you are afraid?

Prayer: "Dear God, please help us, when we are afraid, to choose a course of action that will help others and ourselves move toward freedom despite our fear. [Bring in the special situations the children have mentioned.] Thank you, Lord, Amen."

Song: "Baby Moses"

Registration: Choose classes. Explain what classes will do.

Classes:

Arts and Crafts: Make costumes and/or scenery to correspond with the skit/lesson. The photography group will be taking pictures to make up a slide presentation; they will take pictures of this (arts and crafts) class's reenactment of various skits used in the worship program.

Dance: Make up steps to a preselected recording. This dance will be part of a final program.

Music: Learn songs related to the lesson; the songs will be sung both during worship services and at the final program.

Photography: Learn to operate a 35mm camera, take pictures of reenacted skits and other classroom and outside activities. These pictures will be on slide film and be presented as part of a final program including slide-show production, dance (original), singing and a narrative.

FRUITS AND FLOWERS: HOPE FOR SOCIAL CHANGE

The culmination of our weeks of work comes in our hope for the future. Hopefully, through working together as a family, our teachers, parents, relatives, and children will be more aware of the life around them and will have begun to discover some of the ways that community involvement can begin to change the things that need changing and improve upon the things that are good.

As Christian educators in this urban setting, it is our job to stress what is valuable in the life of the city and to relate it to the values of Christian love, community, and social change.

It is my belief as a Christian educator that the God of the Israelites is the God of today; that same God can and will use the city and its people as instruments in his plan to bring peace to this world.

The author would like to give special thanks to Mary Adebonojo, Debbie Brown, David Gracie, Leslie Grady, Barbara Jenkins, Mary Nelson, Nellie Parker, Jack Studebaker, and many others who worked on the curriculum.

BIBLIOGRAPHY

Anderson, Bernhard. *Understanding the Old Testament,* 2d ed. Englewood Cliffs, N. J.: Prentice-Hall, Inc., 1966.

Douglass, Frederick. *Life and Times of Frederick Douglass.* London: Collier Books, 1962.

Catton, Bruce. "The Dred Scott Case." In *Quarrels that Have Shaped the Constitution,* edited by John A. Garraty. New York: Harper and Row, 1966.

Elkins, Stanley M., *Slavery*. New York: Grosset and Dunlap, 1963. Parts II and III.

Harison, R. K. "Israel in Egypt." *Old Testament Times.* Grand Rapids: William E. Eerdmans, 1970.

Pessin, Deborah, *The Jewish People,* bk. 1, chap. 2. New York: United Synagogue Commission on Education, 1951.

Pritchard, James B., *The Ancient Near East,* pp. 138–166. Princeton: Princeton University Press, 1958.

·8·

Wonder and Response to God

JAN WINTER

In working with children in Christian education, I have come to believe that the key issue is one of engagement. How do we engage our children in the life of faith? How can we help them want for themselves the riches we have found? If only it were simply a matter of *telling* them. But we all know that words fall short and inevitably fail when we are trying to share matters of the heart. Yet we continue to rely on verbal communication of our faith, modeling our religious education efforts after the public schools, with lectures, workbooks, classrooms, age-grading, and content-centered instruction aimed primarily at the child's intellect.

This model may always be an important part of Christian nurture as far as it goes, but it does not go far enough. For we are failing adequately to address our children at the level of "knowing" in which they are most at home: the intuitive or feeling level. When we fail to direct a substantial portion of our teaching to the child's ability to imagine, dream, create, wonder we cannot expect to engage the whole child.

Educational psychologists tell us that humans have two fundamental styles of knowing: one is rational, logical, where new learning is built step by step upon what has been learned before. Thus we learn math, languages, reading, and grammar skills. The second, less understood, is the metaphoric or intuitive mode of knowing. Here the imagination provides the impetus for leaps of understanding that, for instance, allowed the psalmist to know that "The Lord is my shepherd; I shall not want."

As Anglicans, who have long enjoyed the liturgical richness

provided by our Prayer Book and for whom the Sacraments are at the very core of our life together, we have had an ongoing experience of that dimension of worship that transcends the intellect and impels us to come together again and again to feast at the table of our Lord, becoming renewed in ways that we cannot express in words. With such a tradition, we have a special responsibility to break new ground in religious education endeavors in an effort to provide a continuum of excitement and wonder from worship to classroom and back again.

How does one set about accomplishing such a task? I am happy to report that there are many ways—perhaps as many ways as there are parishes with committed and creative people. (I believe that this book provides evidence of that.) My assignment here is to describe in some detail a program that Joseph Wortman and I developed at All-Saints-by-the Sea, Santa Barbara, California.

Feast and Tell was designed for first through sixth graders with adapted sessions for our three-to-five-year-olds. Later it was seminal in the development of sessions for multiage groups, children to adults, which incorporated learning activities into worship settings, culminating each time in the Eucharist. The context, of course, was the freedom for such expression provided by the new liturgy and the emphasis on early admission of children to the Eucharist.

Our title, *Feast and Tell,* comes from the two-fold action of the Eucharist: First comes the Word. We feast on the Word and then experience the Breaking of the Bread. For the "Feasting on Word," the children gather with the teacher to share in the discovery of Christ, the Word. We listen again to the telling of the story, but in a setting especially designed to help us wonder at it in new ways. Elsewhere the congregation is hearing the Epistle, Gospel, and sermon. Then, during the offertory, when the bread and wine are brought to the altar, the children join their parents to break the bread. The ceremony alone spells out without words that something special is happening. The vestments, the candles, the chalice are among the many signs that underscore the children's perception that here is indeed a holy place, a "house of God." Here we are doing something exciting and unique.

The experiences that occasion this awe and wonder in the children must be echoed in the classroom. Each parish works with limitations similar to those that we experienced at All Saints: Teachers who are undertrained, overworked, generally are not appreciated by the children, and are often bored. Then there are the undercommitted parents and children, and the problem of providing some kind of standards and continuity for those who come infrequently. We tried to provide at All Saints a program that would both combat (or neutralize) some of the practical problems and also generate the kind of excitement and anticipation that we felt we must have from the children.

First we planned sessions designed to focus on the Scripture and doctrine inherent in each church season through the use of creative learning experiences. We set up the classrooms as "experience centers," with the rooms gaily decorated each season to stress a different aspect of the seasonal theme. If the season were to be six weeks long, there would be six different rooms to visit, one each week.[1] Before the first week of the season, the children would receive a block of cheerfully designed tickets, which would permit them to visit each of the experience centers, one per week, and have their tickets punched. Teachers taught the same lesson each week of the season, improving and elaborating on it each time, for a different group of children. This format allowed them to spend more time preparing for their session, decorating, gathering materials, reflecting from week to week on new ways to bring the story alive. Sessions were designed so that the theological input spoke for itself without a great deal of formal input from the teacher. Thus the teacher was not put into the position of having to theologize with little background.

For our Pentecost block of sessions, for example, we wanted to provide a way by which the children might receive fresh insights into the presence of the Holy Spirit. We developed a set of six sessions for the Pentecost season, based on experiencing the Holy Spirit through our senses, each session designed to help us sharpen one of our senses, with a sixth session for an "all-my-senses" experience. The "grand design" was to help the children appreciate that all of Creation is a gift from God, and our senses

---

1. Smaller church schools, with no need for as many as six classrooms, have used the session plans one per week or, in some instances, given their children a choice of any of three for the first three weeks, and the other three for the last three weeks of the season.

are his gift to help us know him in all of his Creation, so that we may be led from Creation to the Creator. The following is one of our six lesson plans, the "Touching Experience," which is typical of our approach. Each session plan has the same format: "Wondering Together" is a kind of introductory experience designed to excite the children's interest and lay the groundwork for what is to follow. "Unfolding the Word" is the time for the reading of the Bible story, generally done very simply with just a few words of preparation. (Here we prefer to use the Jerusalem Bible for the beauty of its language and its clarity.) Finally there is the time for "Distilling the Experience," when we try to develop new understanding of what we have done and heard, relate it to what we already know, make it part of us.

THE TOUCHING EXPERIENCE

WONDERING TOGETHER

As the children enter, the leader is seated on a low chair or on the floor and is exploring with her hands and puzzling over a large covered object in front of her. (A sculpture with some special significance should be used. Ours was of a mother holding an infant, with the father kneeling beside them.) The leader invites each child to take a turn exploring it without uncovering it, until each child has had a turn and has made a guess about what it is.

The introduction to the experience should go something like this: "I'm glad you've chosen to come to this room today. You know, this is the time of the year when we in the church celebrate Pentecost. We celebrate Pentecost to remind ourselves of God's gift of the Holy Spirit to the church. But how do we recognize the presence of the Holy Spirit in our lives? We can use our five senses to help us to understand, just as we use them to help us experience everything else in the world."

"What are your five senses?" Children tell leader, who then repeats them slowly with appropriate gestures. "We see, we hear, we touch, etc. All of our senses are a gift from our Father God, the way he has provided for us to experience all that he has made. But we must do our part—we must be alert, sharp, or we'll miss something! And if we are alert, if we sharpen our senses, we will find new ways of experiencing the presence of the Holy Spirit in our lives."

"Today we are going to sharpen our sense of touch!" Now two children are chosen to uncover the sculpture. The children are asked by the leader how they arrived at their guesses; it is hoped they will discover that all of their guesses derived from things that they *felt* as they touched the covered sculpture.

Leader asks, "If you couldn't see or hear, how could you tell whether a friend is happy or sad? Let's try being blindfolded and see whether we can judge a friend's feelings." One volunteer is blindfolded and another is instructed to make either a happy or a sad face. The blindfolded child will have to try to discover the other's expression by touching his face. Others may want to try this.

Now the leader produces the "touching box" (gaily decorated box with hole cut in top to admit a child's hand, insides covered with tactually interesting things), and lets the children take turns feeling the insides. She encourages them to imagine something that feels just like what they are touching, e.g., the prickly feeling of the hairbrush inside the box might remind them of a porcupine or a cactus. As the children have a turn with the box, each may go to the clay or finger-painting table to create the thing he was reminded of, using a medium children love to touch and feel!

For the Bible narration, the children now return to group around the leader. They may want to share what they made and discuss how what they felt inside the box reminded them of the particular object.

UNFOLDING THE WORD

Bible reference is Mark 10:13–16, Jesus blesses the children. Leader reads it from the Jerusalem Bible, remarking at the end, "Our hands help us understand how Jesus can touch us." She encourages the children to take turns blessing each other, ending with discussion of ways in which we touch others to let them know how we feel: hugging, patting a shoulder, shaking hands.

DISTILLING THE EXPERIENCE

During the last minutes of the session, the leader discusses again what the five senses are, stressing the sense of touch. Here she may want to let the children take turns using rubber gloves to try touching things with the sense of touch masked. She may want to introduce the idea of pain and whether it is ever good or useful to experience pain.

Finally the leader leaves the children with these thoughts: "Just as we are able to learn about God's world through touching, we are able to learn more about him through 'inward touching.' Whenever we meet this way, we are changed into being more like him." She may go on to say, "The Bible gives us a picture of how God's Spirit is near us: 'In the beginning God created the heavens and the earth. Now the earth was a formless void [nothing there at all!], there was darkness over the deep, and God's Spirit hovered over the water.' " (Gen. 1:1–2)

Leader may draw attention to the word *hover.* She may ask the children for their ideas about what it means, or ask them to think of things that hover. "God's Spirit is near enough to us to be touched! He is part of us, in fact, because we received him into our lives when we were baptized."

The closing prayer should be simple, making use of insights the children discovered during the "touching experience."

Feast and Tell was designated as a two-year cycle, with hopes that the many other parishes who have adopted it would then take off with their own ideas for still other sessions. Through the blend of excitement and festivity with an underlying serious purpose, the church school can add its contribution to the role of ritual or worship in helping to disclose the sacred to our sight. The children begin to experience more fully their background as part of the family of God, the Church—followers of Christ, who has gone before and calls us to follow.

In this happy framework, a sense of security and belonging grows, for we know there is promised a happy ending for all who follow Christ's way. For Christ means *us* when he says through the Gospels and other writings, "And they lived happily every after."

RESOURCES

Many films, records, books, etc., were used as resources for the various *Feast and Tell* sessions. But none would particularly illuminate our approach.

The one resource that would be most helpful would be *Feast and Tell* itself, with its five introductory chapters explaining in more detail what we tried to do, and its Year I lesson plans. (Year II is also available). Order from: Ms. Jan Winter, 3744 Meru Lane, Santa Barbara, California 93105.

·9·

Family and Intergenerational Education

JANE HILYARD

Family education is a term that we hear often these days in connection with both religious and secular educational programs. Just what is family education anyhow? How does it differ from educational programs that have been going on all these years? In fact, *is* it different and in what way? How does it work? Who may be involved? Who will teach it, or lead groups? Will special training be required for the leaders? Is it a program that we want in our parish?

All these questions and many more have been raised, and are being looked at and considered in many parishes. This section of the book came about in searching for responses to these questions, with the hope that it will provide some answers, some help, and some resources—some possibilities for you to use and encouragement for you to do it!

Family education is an ongoing process. It is happening all the time. It is intentional, in that we try to teach our children that which we believe they will need to know in order to grow and change and to lead full, happy, and complete lives. Partly, it is what we, as members of the Christian community, want to learn about what it means to be a part of that community. Education in our own families is also unintentional in that we learn constructively or destructively from everything we do, whether we think of it consciously as a learning situation or not. Very often in families assumptions are made and acted upon, using our supply of energy and wits and serving no real purpose, thus hindering family growth.

One of the primary goals of intentional family education is to provide opportunities in which families, all kinds—single person families (a single person living alone, or with a friend, or parishioners who may live with families who are not involved with the parish), nuclear families (mom, dad, son, and daughter), single-parent families, extended families (maybe an aunt or grandmother lives with the family unit), blended families (i.e., a second marriage, with children from both first marriages—may gather together to celebrate with each acting out his or her role. The system functions in accordance with the acceptance or nonacceptance of responsibilities by the members of that system. Growth is encouraged by looking at and learning to know the way a specific family's system works. Intentional family education may suggest options and/or alternatives where change may be wanted and needed, helpful and healthful.

A planned family education program identifies and affirms the dynamics that are working for the growth and enrichment of the family. An intentional family education program will provide opportunities for persons and families to examine relationships, communication processes, values, decision-making processes, and conflict-resolution processes. It provides time to make new friends, recognize feelings, discover family strengths, and share learnings.

The foundation of the family education concept is the belief that each individual person is unique and valued, from the youngest to the oldest member of the group. Each individual member contributes to the family system and each has power, regardless of age, within that system. The purpose of intentional family education is to value and affirm each individual, to heighten the awareness of each individual, to recognize the power and related contribution of each member of the family, and to explore options and alternatives for individuals within the system and for the system itself.

There is a variety of forms a family education program may take. In all programs, events for the families' experience and learning are designed according to the identified hopes and expectations of the people involved. The learning takes place in the experience, the doing of the events, and is recognized—"owned"—in the sharing or the reflection on that experience. When family education takes place in the church, it incorporates

Christian values and allows for Christian growth and nurture as well as family growth and nurture.

A "FIRST-TIME" FAMILY EDUCATION PROGRAM—ONE CHURCH'S STORY

In the early spring a few years back, the rector and a committee of self-appointed volunteers wanted to do something about the current religious education program in the parish. It was a program that was tired. Attendance had hit bottom and willing teachers were scarcer than hen's teeth. Several members of the parish who were interested in a revitalized program met several times, working with ideas, curriculum materials, and resources from the church library. After much tossing around of ideas and suggestions, we identified a need for a program that would include everyone, all ages together—a multifamily intergenerational program. We did not want to leave anyone out and we did not want to separate the program into various age categories.

As we talked about the kind of program we wanted, we began to look at the resources we had. Nothing fit. Then into our midst came a brochure advertising a new Christian education curriculum—*Family,* by Maureen Gallagher, published by Paulist Press. It was an answer to our prayers! It fit. It was (almost) just what we wanted, we thought.

Many people put in lots and lots of hours as we began to adapt the curriculum to our situation. We took the material designed for a two-hour once-a-month session and adapted it to fit a one-hour every-Sunday-morning meeting. The material was conveniently divided into units, with each unit providing about six weeks' material. We started the program in early September with seven family groups, about twenty-five persons in each group. There were four to six families in each group, including single-person families.

Reaction to the Family Program showed us that almost half of the people involved really responded to and enjoyed the program, looked forward to the session each week, and voiced hopes of continuing this type of program in the future. The other half of the group was not so favorable in its response. We did a survey in the spring to gather data on the Family Program. The results of the survey supported the reactions. We learned that there was need for *both* a more traditional group-graded program and a multifamily program.

Those of us on the planning committee made and acted upon the assumption that everyone (in the parish) was as interested and eager for the Family Program as we were. The committee was a large one, a good representation of the parish. We learned a truth we must reckon with in all our planning for any religious education program: All of us are not in the same place at the same time and cannot respond in the same way to any one program.

A Christian education program must, as nearly as possible, provide for the multiple needs of the persons in the congregation. Our experience showed us that a total multifamily program could not replace a more traditional group-graded program, certainly not in our parish and probably not in any parish. At the same time, our experience clearly indicated that there were definite needs for growth and enrichment programs. Multifamily programs are ideally suited to short-term (eight to ten week) series and make excellent offerings in connection with a total parish Christian educaiton program.

There are many ways to add family programs to any parish. You may want to start with a whole-parish family day—perhaps a potluck lunch following the service on Sunday and an afternoon of games, singing, and folk dancing. Plan for a parish-family weekend at a nearby camp or conference center, with some time reserved for intentional family learning and sharing, and some valuable time to be a community of Christians, rejoicing in the knowledge of God's love. Create a parish-family festival, possibly to begin the season of Advent or to celebrate Penetcost.

AN EXPERIENCE IN MULTIFAMILY EDUCATION

In order to provide a clearer picture of what multifamily and intergenerational education looks like, I would like to share with you my experience in working with a small downtown parish.

The parish is not large, perhaps as many as a hundred families. As it is a "downtown" parish, it reflects a wide range of families in its membership. There are many single-person families, as well as nuclear families, single-parent families, extended families, and blended families. It is the kind of parish (like yours) that provides a real challenge for those members who are charged with the development of a creative and stimulating religious education program in which all may participate.

An out-of-town weekend was planned as a total parish program. About half of the parish, or more, came for the weekend at the seaside church conference center. The agenda for the weekend included time for a structured multifamily program as well as time for worship, shared meals, relaxation, and play.

The structured family time provided the opportunity for each family to have some time together to reflect on all the "treasures" contained in each member and in each family. The family members together made lists of some of the things that were "special" about each person, and things that were special about each family. They listed that which was particularly important to them, such as:

1. Other persons, not in their immediate family but especially important to them.
2. Important and special places—maybe their home, or a favorite camp-site, or grandma's house.
3. Pets—an important part of the family, each special in its own way.
4. Roots and family ties—particularly family histories.
5. Rites, special celebrations, traditions, rituals: "We always have chocolate cake for Dad's birthday!" etc.
6. Songs, games, stories that your family particularly enjoys.
7. Activities—things that involve every member of the family in recreation or adventure.
8. Other: something unique and extra-special about your family.

After each family had made lists of their treasures, each was given an empty box, scissors, colored paper, old magazines, glue, and magic markers. Using all these materials and the skill and creative energy of each person, they created a "family treasure chest" representing themselves and the items on their lists.

When the chests were completed (the time needed to list the

treasures and construct the treasure chest is about forty-five minutes) the families all gathered together in a big circle, their treasure chests in front of them. Each family, with each person participating, had the opportunity to share its treasures with the members of their community gathered there. The affirmation of each person within each family, and the affirmation of each family as a part of the total parish community was powerful to witness. A "glue" was made that day that united this parish community in a positive and dynamic way. These people began to be acquainted, to really know and care about each other. They became a family—a sturdy cohesive unit recognizing the value and importance of each individual as a part of the whole.

This activity took most of the day on Saturday. It does take time for each family to share its treasures with the whole group, but it is time spent in the best way. In allowing the time needed for this to happen, each individual is valued for the special unique person he or she is, and each family is valued as a part of this particular community of God's own family.

With this weekend as a beginning, a foundation of a multifamily education program in the parish, a new venture into Christian Education was opened to them.

The parish vestry voted to support a family leadership training program for three members who wanted to serve as leaders in a program for their congregation. After their training they developed a series of multifamily education programs for the parish. They began with a program for Advent. It consisted of a two-hour session once each week for four weeks. Several families, including some single-person families, participated. Advent themes and preparation for Christmas provided the content material for this short series.

The positive response to the Advent program inspired the group leaders to develop a second multifamily education program series. Starting in January, it continued on a two-hour, once-a-week meeting for eight weeks. There were still more families interested in a multifamily program, and in response to them a third series was projected for later in the spring. These family group meetings took place on a evening in the middle of the week, and were separate from the Sunday morning program.

In order to allow for the full participation of each person, the size of the group should be kept to about twenty-five members. This allows for the maximum participation of each person in the group.

Ideally, a multifamily education group would be made up of a young family with young children; a second family a little older, whose children are also a little older than the first; a third and fourth family both with teen-age children; with perhaps an aunt or uncle or grandparent of one of the families; and one or two single-person families. The ideal is rarely, if ever, possible; but what you look for and hope for is an age continuum, so the younger children have older children models, the teen-agers have young adult models, and the younger couple have older couple or older single-person models. Teen-agers really need to have other teen-agers in the group, and young adults are really important to the teen-ager, too.

The families who responded to the eight-week series agreed on their part to be there for each session. They all agreed to begin their time together with a meal, starting at 6 P.M. at the parish hall with a brown-bag supper, coffee, and juice provided. They all agreed to participate and to be punctual. The leaders agreed that they would plan activities and group work accommodating as nearly as possible the stated needs and expectations of the members of the group. They all agreed that they would stick to the stated closing time, 8 P.M. Whether it is called a contract, agreement, or covenant, it is important that these steps not be taken for granted, assumed, or overlooked. Agreeing to the outlines and structure of the group allows for members to take responsibility for themselves to "own" membership in the group and to participate on their own terms.

Before the first meeting of the group, the group leaders gathered information from the members to determine what direction their planning would take. In this case a brief questionnaire was filled out by each person in each family. The younger children answered the questions, too, with either a parent or one of the group leaders acting as scribe for them.

An interview may be used instead of a questionnaire or it may be used in conjunction with a written questionnaire. The object is to obtain as much information as you can about the members of the group and what they want and expect to have happen in the group.

A simple questionnaire might include these questions: your name, age, and grade in school; what you especially like about your family; whom you talk to when you have something really important to share; favorite song or game or sport that the family does together; what you hope to have happen in this group; what you would like to share with the group, such as playing guitar, etc.; and what you would like to learn together.

The information gathered from the families indicated that they would like to work toward better communication with each other in their family, and family-to-family, building toward a stronger community of their total church congregation.

Communication within the family includes a wide range of possibilities of what family members might work on specifically. Some of the items that were named by this group were family roles and rules, family systems, and affirmations of persons within the family.

The first session was devoted to getting acquainted with one another, person with person and family with family. Getting acquainted with the program, looking ahead, general plans for the next seven sessions were discussed by the members of the group. They explored the space that would be used for their working and playing together. They discussed and planned together the setting up and cleaning up responsibilities and who would take care of these for each session. Discussion also touched on who in each family would take responsibility in getting ready to come to the family sessions. Usually Mom has the job of getting the food ready, so the group discussed what other options might be workable—who would help with what, so that all could benefit from their cooperation.

Immediately after the first session, when the cleanup was done and the last family had gone home, the group leaders used the next hour or so to get ready for the next session. They began by talking about how each of them felt about this session, how it had developed, and what they felt about the participation of the members. They shared their observations of the group. What they had heard members say and the behavior they had observed.

Using this information, plus what they already knew about the group, they planned the next session.

The group leaders had observed active participation by every member of the group and they agreed that there was a good climate of trust beginning to build in this group. Everyone had been eager to share something about themselves with the group. There was happy anticipation about being together the next week. Using this knowledge and the earlier identified request for learning communication skills, the group leaders planned an activity for the next session that would allow the participants to look at their roles in the family and to share this information with members of their own families and with others from the total group in a simulated family.

A simulated or "made-up" family allows each person to experience a different model from those in his own family. Mom is still Mom, to another group, and Dad is still Dad, a daughter is a daughter, and a son a son, but each has the opportunity to experience these persons in a family new and different from his own family. Seeing and experiencing a Mom operating in a different way (because although she really is a Mom, she is Mom in a different system), her sharing of who she is, of the way she is Mom in her own system can be very rewarding to the group.

In the next session, using an exercise called "Hats," everyone was asked to take a few minutes and think of all the things they did in their families. For example:

> *Son:* Dog-feeder, garbage-emptier, floor-sweeper, short-stop.
> *Daughter:* Baby-sitter, cookie-baker, musicmaker, reader.
> *Mom:* Chief cook, taxi-driver, nurse, reader, nagger, swim coach.
> *Dad:* Bill-payer, garbage-emptier, golfer, ball-player.

When all the roles had been determined, each person was asked to make a "hat" for each role named. Use strips of poster card, about three inches wide and about twenty-seven inches long, and magic markers. By cutting or tearing at the top of one end and the bottom of the other, the strip can be made into a circle; cut ends fit into each other, and voilà! A "hat."

Everyone makes all the hats they can think of for themselves. These are shared in simulated families and then in actual families. The sharing includes: what the hat (role) is; the hat I like best and how I feel when I'm wearing (doing) it; the hat I like least and how I feel about it; the hat I wear most often and how I feel about it.

As the hats are discussed, family members get new information about themselves and about each other. Often the recognition of how one feels about a role comes in the sharing of this role and the feeling it generates as they talk about it. By sharing first in a simulated family group, the speakers get new insights that they will want to share in their own family. The roles that are part of the family's living together (their system) can be seen in a new and different way. The sharing of feelings is particularly important. Perhaps negotiations can be made within the family for exchanging roles or eliminating unnecessary ones. There is a climate of openness, and the possibility for growth.

As the families gathered together for closing prayers, they sang "He's Got the Whole World in His Hands," singing a chorus for each family, i.e., "He's got the Jones family in His Hands," etc.

Planning for each of the ensuing sessions in this series was done following the earlier-mentioned process. Information was gathered, the behavior observed, and the learnings identified in the group were discussed by the group leaders. On the basis of the information gathered and additional questions and expectations stated by members of the group, the leaders determined what the next step would be. A decision was made about what work the group might next do to build on the results of the prior session. They bore in mind the initial agreement made with the group and the stated hopes and expectations for the life and growth and enrichment of the group totally and of the members individually.

The planning for the final session requires special attention to the fact that it *is* the final session. Some special celebration needs to be organized to recognize this fact. Everyone in the group will want to help plan for this important event. It is necessary to allow some time in the next-to-last session to plan this celebration and designate who will be responsible for which part of it.

In this particular group a potluck supper was organized. One of the members of the group, a widow who lived near the church, offered her apartment for the occasion. The activity for the evening was to complete the banner that had been designed as a gift for the parish hall. The last part of the evening was to be a worship service, including reading Evening Prayer and singing the songs that had become favorites of the group. All members of the group would have the opportunity to offer prayers of thanksgiving for their life in the group. This final session would also be an opportunity for each to affirm one another in new friendship and loving relationship within the body of Christ.

As the series went on, each session building on the previous one, the group and what they were about became more meaningful and fruitful for each of the persons involved. As they all became better and better acquainted, the climate of trust was enhanced not only for the individuals within families but among all the families in the group. A common bond of their life within their parish community was strengthened. The goals and expectations for better communication with family members and with other families were met. New learnings were discovered and shared. New friendships celebrated. God's love was known among them.

THE EIGHT-WEEKS SESSIONS

AN OUTLINE FOR THE EIGHT-WEEKS PROGRAM:

Format (agenda) for all sessions:

- 6:00 P.M. opening; grace; supper
- song or game
- structured activity or exercise
- reflection on exercise or activity
- song or game
- clean up
- 8 P.M. prayers; closing

followed by planning time for group leaders

QUESTIONS FOR GATHERING DATA—INTERVIEW OR QUESTIONNAIRE:

1. What do you have the most fun doing with your family?
2. What do you like about your family?
3. What is the happiest part of your day?
4. When you have something special to share, to whom do you go?
5. What do you want to have happen for your family in this program?

6. What are your favorite free-time activities?
7. What do you wish for, for your family?

SESSIONS PLAN:

First Session

Purpose: To get acquainted with one another and with the total group.

Exercise/Activity: Flower Garden Mural; agreement to Family Education Program (contracting)

Second Session

Purpose: To continue to get acquainted; to look at family roles and rules.

Exercise/Activity: Hats; discussion in simulated family and own family.

Third Session

Purpose: To provide a tool to help us:

- to recognize our feelings
- to share our feelings
- to be responsible for our feelings

Exercise/Activity: Faces; discussion in simulated family and own family; Song—"*Got to Get in Touch with the Way that I Feel*" (from *Hi God,* by Rev. Carey Landry and Carol Jean Kinghorn, published by North American Liturgy Resources, 1973). (See Table 9.1.)

Fourth Session

Purpose: To affirm each individual; to recognize each as part of the total group.

Exercise/Activity: Life-size figures (See Table 9.2.)

Fifth Session

Purpose: To explore the family as a system; to affirm each family

Exercise/Activity: Family Mobile (See Table 9.3.)

Sixth Session

Purpose: To look at rules in our own family and in our family of origin (grandparents).

Exercise/Activity: film, *The Adventures of an Asterisk,* by John Hubley, distributed by Contemporary Films; discussion of family rules, now and in comparison to rules in family of origin.

Seventh Session

Purpose: To work together to plan and begin banner, gift for Church; to plan final session, worship and celebration.

Exercise/Activity: Brainstorm ideas for banner, choose design, determine working groups and tasks (for banner).

Eighth Session

Purpose: To create banner; to celebrate our life together as a group.

Exercise/Activity: Planned potluck supper; finish banner; worship and closing.

TABLE 9.1: FACES

An exercise that gives us the opportunity to learn about and share our feelings.

Total Group: Brainstorm and put up on newsprint or chalkboard a vocabulary of words that we can use to describe feelings.

Each Person: Draw a happy face, a sad face, and an angry face (paper plates are good for this exercise).

Discussion: In simulated families and then in own family.

Tell the members in your group some of the things that make you feel happy, sad, and angry. Share with them how you feel when you wear each face. Family members respond with how they feel when you wear that face.

TABLE 9.2: LIFE-SIZE FIGURES

An exercise that helps us to become aware of our uniqueness and affirm individuality.

Needed: a length of newsprint, life-size, for each person.

Partners: Each one draws the outline of the other on a sheet of newsprint. Each person draws in his own features and clothes on the figure. Each then shares the following information about himself (it may be written or verbal): Some of the things I can do; Some of the ways I'm like my family; Some of the things people can learn from me.

TABLE 9.3: FAMILY MOBILE

An exercise that provides the opportunity to explore the family as a system, and to affirm each member of that family.

Needed: pieces of cardboard, old magazines, colored paper, scissors, glue, assorted sticks or pieces of doweling, and string. Each person in the family chooses a piece of cardboard, shapes it, and decorates it to be self-representing, including name. A line may be strung across the room on which to hang the mobiles. Each family then puts their mobile together, beginning with Mom and Dad. As the pieces representing them are being hung up, all share with the family how they adjust to the other, forming the beginning of their family system. Then the children add their pieces, from oldest to youngest, and each shares about the readjustment necessary with each addition. Family pets should be included, as we often have to make adjustments with the addition of, and sometimes the death of, a pet.

The family mobile provides a good tool to represent the balance and imbalance that may be present in our family system. It is also an object that the family may take home with them, to value as a reminder of who each is in their family system.

LEADERSHIP TRAINING FOR FAMILY EDUCATION PROGRAMS

There are many questions concerning the leadership of Family Education Programs. Who will teach family education? What are the necessary qualifications for those who will teach or lead groups? What kind of training is needed, wanted, and helpful? Are training programs available?

These questions were my own as I first began to be involved in family education programs a few years ago. I had taught in the public school system, first and second grades, when I was newly married and fresh out of college. That experience was most helpful to me. Then our own family expanded with the birth of a daughter and then a son. All of the wonderful and traumatic experiences of parenthood helped me to realize how much I didn't know and how very much I wanted to learn. The years of working with various groups— Brownie Scouts, Cub Scouts, PTA, teaching Sunday School, volunteer enrichment programs in the public schools—all these were educational for me. In many ways these activities were rewarding, but unsatisfactory, too, in revealing areas in which I needed and wanted to learn more.

Eager for new adventures in learning experiences, I took part in a Communicating Arts Lab at our church's conference center. The participants—those who responded to the advertisement in the diocesan newspaper—came to "spend a week together to build community." We were a mixed combination: an arthritic retired schoolteacher; a recently divorced woman; some whole families and parts of other famlies, including three tough-looking teen-agers. Our youngest member was a precocious almost four-year-old boy; and the oldest was a dear lady who had sixty-seven years' living experience to share with us. The fantastic thing was that we did indeed become a community. We became a family. Our learning, hoping, worrying, working, eating, playing, and worshipping together united us in a family bond, a relationship that is still alive and special.

That experience was multifamily intergenerational education.

Since that time I have looked for and responded to situations that provided the opportunity to work with and to be involved in multifamily and intergenerational groups. Most of these experiences have been within religious educational volunteer programs.

I found some very helpful training in human relations offered through diocesan training programs; then some additional training in design skills and personal growth workshops. I took part in a Family Clustering Leadership training workshop led by Dr. Margaret Sawin of Family Clustering, Inc., Rochester, N.Y. More recently I participated in a seminar with Virginia Satir—Family Education for Growth and Health. I have worked on the planning team and staff of an ecumenically sponsored Family Education Workshop for the last three summers. This workshop offers training opportunities for those who would like to work as leaders in Family Education groups, and it offers a structured family education experience.

Among my most valued and most used resources are the books written by Virginia Satir. I find them to be clearly concise, containing much that is useful and helpful. I strongly recommend her work: *Peoplemaking*, published Palo Alto, Calif.: Science and Behavior Books, 1972; *Making Contact,* published Millbrae, Calif.: Celestial Arts, 1976; *Self Esteem,* also published by Celestial Arts, 1975; and *Changing with Families,* vol. l, written with Richard Bandler and John Grinder, published Palo Alto, Calif.: Science and Behavior Books, 1976.

A new book, written especially for those persons who are interested in family education will be published in the fall of 1978. It has been written with love and great care by two very special people. The combination of their years of experience in the church and in family and intergeneratioal education shines brightly throughout this book: *Becoming Family,* by Jeanette Benson, S. P. and Jack L. Hilyard. To be published by St. Mary's College Press, Winona, Minnesota.

RESOURCES AND BIBLIOGRAPHY

In describing some experiences with family education groups, several songs, exercises, games, books, etc., have been mentioned. These are just some of the resources that are used in Family Education groups. There are a number of other resources. The most important resource is often assumed or overlooked. It is yourself. You, and every person involved as members of the family group, are the most valuable resource available. Each of us has a number of years' experience in living, in growing, and in sharing and caring. We all have skills and talents and abilities. We *all* have these. We all need to share what we have. We all want to do this, too. At the same time, we all are shy, reluctant to offer what we think may be a "dumb" suggestion. Stronger, though, is the need to share. We need to share with each other who we are, what we feel, what we think, what we care about, what we hope for. In a very real sense, this is what family education is all about. It is to let each of us know that our ideas are wanted, that our skills and abilities, whatever they may be, are valuable and needed by our total community, our whole family.

Other things that we think of more quickly as resources are the materials which we use as we do our work together in groups. Newsprint and marking pens and masking tape, paper and paints, old magazines and Elmer's Glue are basic equipment to almost any group work. All of us who have worked in any education program within the church have found sources for materials, especially those things that may be "recycled": empty cardboard boxes from the local supermarket, trimmings or overages from the local print shop, and millends from fabric manufacturers.

Children's literature is a rich resource for family education materials. Many books that are written for children have great potential for family learning and enrichment. The following is a list of some of the ones that I have found most useful:

Leichman, Seymour. *The Boy Who Could Sing Pictures.* New York: Holt, Rinehart, and Winston, 1973. The story of a miracle—and of a loving relationship between father and son.

Lionni, Leo. *A Color of His Own.* New York: Pantheon, 1975. Very simply told, the story of looking for an identity of self.

Lionni, Leo. *Fish Is Fish.* New York: Pinwheel Books, 1974. A beautifully simple story about being who you are, where you are, and the rightness of that.

Lionni, Leo. *Frederick.* New York: Pinwheel Books, 1973. A tender and beautiful story about a sensitive mouse and his sharing of gifts in his community family—about love and affirmation.

Lionni, Leo. *Pezzettino.* New York: Pantheon, 1975. Pezzettino is so small he is convinced that he must be a piece of somebody else. A wiseman helps him discover the truth.

Lionni, Leo. *Swimmy.* New York: Pantheon, 1963. A beautiful story about sharing who you are and the importance of family and community.

Lionni, Leo. *Tico and the Golden Wings.* New York: Pinwheel Books, 1975. A story about being the same and being different, a recognition and affirmation of self.

McDermott, Gerald. *Arrow to the Sun.* New York: Viking Press, 1974. The story of a boy in search for his father, and the sharing of his father's love.

Morse, Ann and Charles. *Whobody There?* Winona, Minn.: St. Mary's College Press, 1971. About those people in our lives who are important to us—those we love, who love us.

Ness, Evaline. *Sam, Bangs and Moonshine.* New York: Holt, Rinehart, and Winston, 1966. A very useful, well-written imaginative story about communication in a family.

Sendak, Maurice. *Where the Wild Things Are.* New York: Scholastic Book Service, 1963. About a little boy, a great imagination, and the expressing and communicating of feelings.

·10·

Christians and the Hungry: Action and Reflection in Education

STEPHEN COMMINS

[The following chapter is an example of the correlation of action and Christian education. Action and involvement is key in the educational process. The development of this hunger curriculum illustrates that the action of the congregation itself is part of the educational process.]

INTRODUCTION

The purpose of this curriculum is to provide a foundation and guide for parishes that are interested in studying and responding to the needs of the hungry. This is not a "canned" program that is to be adopted as is by any or every parish. Rather it is an attempt to develop a road map for those interested in developing programs on a parish level—programs that go beyond a brief study and into a long-term commitment to work on hunger concerns.

Following the headlines in 1974 and 1975, many churches sought to develop hunger programs or to learn more about the issue. Some of these programs have lasted for several years, but many have faded in short periods of time. Too often people have felt that they have "done" hunger because of a fast, a hunger walk, or one study series. Yet as the issue of hunger has vanished from the front pages and nightly news, some churches have begun to dig deeper. They have tried to prepare for the long haul. For, in effect, the faces of the hungry challenge the church to *be* the church, the community of Christ to those in need. Thus any home-grown curriculum must be part of the congregation's whole life and emerge from the people themselves.

The four main sections of this curriculum are metaphors of a garden or backyard farm. This has been chosen for two reasons. The first is that, as with growing food or flowers, a hunger program must have a living and dynamic process. It must be continually tended and examined. The second is that the harvest is an essential aspect of the program. It is not enough to have had a four- or six-week study about hunger. The continuation of this concern is the result of a carefully planned and lively, involving experience. These are the fruits by which the program will be known.

I. THE PREPARATION (CLEARING THE LAND)

The decision to launch a parish program of study and response to hunger means that a commitment of significance has been made by the congregation. For the planning and even the program itself should only be seen as a beginning. Thus the involvement and participation of parishioners in various ways must be sought from the start. This participation must be a priority issue for the leadership of the parish and those interested in the issue.

Who should be involved in the initial planning?

For the first planning event, a representative cross section of the parish should be gathered. This group should be invited by the clergy, wardens, and the one or two people who have been selected as facilitators of the planning process (and it should be clear from the start that those whose skills have them facilitating planning are not being committed or "stuck" with running the curriculum itself). One way to develop the planning group is to have the clergy, wardens (or selected vestry representatives), and facilitators make a list of parishioners they feel comprise a cross section of the parish. The length will vary with the size of the parish, but it should be at least ten and could be up to fifty or sixty.

When the group first meets for an evening session, the purpose of the evening needs to be clearly explained: for the developing of a program for the entire parish—not just looking at a five-week study (or whatever length), but an inclusive design that includes

Sunday morning (worship and education), various ongoing parish organizations, and whatever service programs are already in existence. Then the group needs to ask a number of questions.

What is education?

a. Is it primarily passive?
b. How does it change us?
c. What would be a learning situation?
d. What experiences will change us?
e. What risks are involved?

Then, as the group prepares to work in subgroups of five or six, they should also consider their planning with several questions/goals in mind:

1. Why are people hungry?
2. Where are people hungry? (particularly locally)
3. What are we doing now about hunger?
4. What should we be doing in the future?
5. How is God calling this particular parish to learn and to grow in meeting the needs of the hungry?

The responsibility of the small groups is to come up with as many different ideas as possible. For the rest of the evening they are to list without discussion (except for brief explanation) ideas that might be part of the hunger curriculum. Listed below are examples that should be seen as only part of what could be done (in fact, one parish had over 150 different ideas from the first night):

- soup night
- fasting
- hunger walk
- film series
- penitential worship
- the Bible and hunger
- visiting a community service center
- a food-basket collection every Sunday
- prayer vigil
- forming a Bread for the World group or joining Impact
- vegetarian meals

- nutrition education
- no doughnuts after church on Sunday
- monthly hunger pledges
- studying a particular country
- reading *Food First,*[1] *Bread for the World,*[2] or *Rich Christians in an Age of Hunger.*[3]

All the suggestions that are made in the small groups may be discussed briefly with the whole gathering at the end of the evening. Following compline or a time of prayer and sharing, one individual can make a list of all ideas offered from the groups. This list can be mailed to all those who took part in the meeting for reflection prior to the subsequent meeting (preferably the next week). In addition, the Sunday bulletin could contain an insert that would explain what had happened at the first planning meeting and would encourage others both to submit ideas and/or to attend the second planning meeting.

What about obstacles? (Or, removing the boulders.)

Any effort at clearing the land will occasionally encounter boulders or rocky ground. These range from apathy and indifference on the part of significant parts of the congregation to hostility towards the whole curriculum. Some may feel that the church has already had programs on hunger or that there was a soup dinner last year and it just made people feel guilty. Others may argue that the issues are too political or that the church should concern itself with "spiritual matters." Such obstacles need not be dismissed or crushed without a response to the people concerned. This may be a pastoral matter that requires leadership from the laity and not the clergy alone. Also, it may require a reaffirmation of commitment to the program by the parish, and this can be a good way of strengthing commitment.

Be not anxious: If a dozen Christians were gathered together and asked to respond to the word *hunger* with one or two different words, such words as anxiety, guilt, and frustration would be

---

1. Joseph Collins and Francis Moore Lappé, *Food First* (Boston: Houghton Mifflin, 1977).

2. Arthur Simon, *Bread for the World* (Grand Rapids, Michigan: Eerdmans, 1975).

3. Ronald Sidec, *Rich Christians in an Age of Hunger* (Downers Grove, Illinois: Inter-Varsity Press, 1977).

among the responses. Thus it is important that leadership in parishes be sensitive to the guilt that well-intentioned people feel when faced with the seemingly insoluble dilemmas of world hunger. A response to their feelings will be to emphasize positive programs already in existence, the possibilities of change, and the image of Christian responsibility not through guilt but service. One way to do this is to focus on local projects that will serve to encourage a sense of hope and provide a different image than a sea of hungry, helpless faces.

Obstacles will arise from many different sources. Some will come from defensiveness, some from a hazy or distorted understanding of the church's mission, and some from failures in the past. The development of a parish hunger program needs to be deeply rooted in the Gospel and the church's spiritual life. It will live only as part of a worshiping and praying community. Obstacles that arise to the hunger curriculum should be seen in the context of the parish's total life. And they should be met as part of the renewal and the discipleship of the whole community.

II. PLANTING THE SEEDS

The second meeting of the curriculum planning group will be devoted to moving from an open list of ideas to the beginning of a coherent program. It is important to recognize that no single series of events will be able to encompass the diversity of possible ideas. No one need feel slighted if his particular project is not chosen at this time. This experience should lead to more in the future. (The list of ideas from the first meeting should be saved for use at another time, for the ideas not chosen the first time as well as for a record of the first planning process.)

To begin the meeting, groups can be assigned or voluntarily picked by the participants. Possible divisions might be (and there are more than those below):

1. Education/Action/Worship/Life-style
2. Children's program/Education/Sunday morning/Nutrition
3. Community service/Political action/Education/Worship
4. Life-style/Worship/Political action/Children's program

These groups are then given the task of looking at all the ideas that have been suggested and seeing which ones they think fit into their particular category. Once their list has been compiled (and there will always be an overlap between two groups), the group then begins to rank the ideas in priority. That way, depending on the length of the program, the number of weeks involved, and the time required for each activity, they will be able to focus on what is feasible for this curriculum. In addition, an important series of questions can be asked at this point in the planning:

1. How will these programs and ideas move toward answering the five questions/goals in the introductory section?

2. Are these ideas interesting enough so that the people not involved in the planning process will participate in the program?

3. Are there ideas that will help motivate members of the parish to continue this concern after the initial curriculum has been completed?

The questions of how to and what motivates people is an essential one, which must be faced as the curriculum is being developed. It is not enough (and sometimes is quite paralyzing) to pour out facts and information about hunger. The participants must be converted to a deeper sense of the church as the servant community. This has at least three components. A sense of Scripture and Christian commitment is the lifeblood of the program. The power of the praying and worshiping community is at the core of the entire experience. And, the problem of hunger cannot remain on the impersonal level. To succeed, a curriculum needs to come face to face with the poor and with their lives—it is from the experience of meeting the poor that a Christian response will be enriched and inevitably deepened.

Each parish will have its own area in which to meet the poor, but some initial questions will help in this process:

1. Who are the poor in our community?
2. What is being done in ways of assistance to the poor?
3. What factors help to perpetuate poverty in the community?
4. How are the poor themselves involved in changing their lives?
5. What has this parish done already in this area?
6. What can we do now? (initial suggestions)

These questions will have more applicability in some groups than in others, but the need for motivation remains the same. Other groups could ask such questions as:

1. How does our life-style affect our commitment to the poor?
2. What scriptural resources speak to justice and concern for the poor?
3. What can we do to help ourselves through changing our diets?
4. How can I deepen my own faith through a penitential discipline?

And each group should do the following:

1. What resource people are available in the parish? (list)
   a. teaching
   b. group leadership
   c. devotional work
   d. community service
2. What resource people are available in the community?
   a. nutritionist
   b. community service worker
   c. film librarian
   d. co-op organizer

The decisions on whom to contact and how to use these contacts is part of the life a homegrown curriculum takes on for itself. One area where the decisions are especially localized is in the area of touching the lives of the poor. It will have a different shape in each parish and will vary in communities. What follows are descriptions of what one parish did, and how another parish, in a very different situation, could do something with the same goals. (While the following relates specifically to the poor, these models can apply to other areas of concern.)

Santa Monica, California:

1. A presentation on a program that works with the poor and hungry, especially children, in Tijuana.
2. The preparation for solicitation of food at local supermarkets for the hungry.

3. Spend the evening at supermarkets and return to the church to share experiences with the other groups.

4. Presentation by a nun who works with the Spanish-speaking community in Santa Monica.

5. Presentation by a Chicano who works with a community service agency in which a few parishioners are involved.

(In addition, a group of parishioners spends the weekend with the project in Tijuana and then shares this experience with the congregation. This is the fifteenth time a group from the church has worked on the project in Tijuana, but this has provided the work with its broadest audience and greatest interest.)

Hudson Valley, New York (removed from any large urban area):

1. Where are the poor in our community? (and in our own parish?)
   - the elderly
   - the transient
   - migrant farm workers
   - poor farmers
   - the unemployed, especially those out of work because of shifting business patterns or an industry closing

2. What is being done for/with the poor now?

3. Who, if anyone, speaks for the poor in this community?

4. What can we do (short term) to help the poor and hungry in our community?

5. What can we do (long term) to help the poor/hungry in our community?

(The above ideas should not rule out the use of films or filmstrips, guest speakers or simulation games, but the experiential component is critical to the program's success.)

Two other areas are important in a parish hunger curriculum. The first is the parallel development of a children's program for the duration of the hunger study (and beyond?). There are many ways in which children are able to understand hunger issues and to participate in the program. They should be involved in the planning process, realizing that there are many more ideas than a group could cover in any course of study. These include:

- filmstrips on self-help projects
- food collections and delivery
- nutrition education
- meeting children from other communities
- a presentation on a simple project that the children could support from ongoing contributions
- role playing
- food solicitation at supermarkets
- Bible stories

Equally essential is the role of the curriculum coordinator. This is *not* the same as giving someone the responsibility for developing the curriculum or coordinating the process of curriculum development (this belongs to the initial committee). The coordinator needs to be in contact with the various subgroups in order to facilitate the parish's program. This means that one central calendar, time line, list of needs, etc., can be kept by the coordinator to avoid confusion. It is this tentatively complete list that should be the beginning of the involvement of the entire parish.

III. NURTURING THE CROP

Gaining Congregational Support and Involvement

Between the initial core group and the congregation as a whole lie several potential gaps. The first is the distance between the enthusiasm and the commitment that exist within the initial planning group—particularly a small group that has gained a certain vision and spirit from its participation in the planning process. In addition the congregation may have only the haziest idea of what the hunger curriculum is about. It is essential that those who have taken part in the planning be able to translate and share their ideas and hopes with their fellow parishioners.

One initial strength for the program is that the participation of parishioners in the planning provides a built-in core group committed to the curriculum and to the parish's investment in it. It should also mean that a representative planning group will personally be in contact with the broadest possible spectrum of parishioners. The personal recruitment is as necessary as the advertising through posters, flyers, and bulletin inserts. Members of the planning group should have the opportunity to speak at Sunday services and perhaps even develop a lay sermon (or several brief presentations that share their convictions). This will help the whole parish family in seeing the "home-grown" nature of the hunger program and the enthusiasm that has been generated. The program can then be seen as a mission calling to all.

Keeping the Programs Moving

A "burn-out" factor can be avoided if responsibility for the weekly programs is shared as broadly as possible. If preparation for dinners, worship, main programs, service projects, etc., is in the hands of a number of individuals, pairs, or small groups, then no one person or few people will be exhausted by the end of the experience. The program coordinator will have succeeded in his or her role by supporting each particular effort but not by taking it on personally. The clergy and resource people who have been enlisted should serve as examples of how to "plug in" to a specific area of concern without being involved in everything. The worship and sharing times are especially important in this regard. The support and nurture of the faith community is the lifeline that helps keep the hardest worker from becoming isolated or cut off from his or her time for God and for others. A sense of pastoral concern interest is part of the servant community. We cannot seek to serve others if we allow those in our own midst to be wrecked physically or emotionally in their efforts to effect program development.

Weeds (Complaints, Breakdowns, etc.)

The difficulties or complications that arise within an individual program will be unique to that parish and to the people involved. But there are ways in which the hurts can be healed, breakdowns fixed, and complaints heard. A spirit of openness is a key aspect of the program, along with admission that this is a learning for all, including the planners. If some fail in their responsibility for a component of the curriculum, they need the forgiveness of the community. If an individual or group finds an aspect of the program to be controversial or offensive, they need to know that they have been heard. But, at the same time, it should be recognized that peace will not be purchased by ignoring controversy or differences. Churches need to be honest about the conflict that can be a part of social change and not to be innocuous or lacking in courage. No hunger program can possibly make everyone happy or meet every preconception. But even as the church does not shrink from conflict, the leaders of the curriculum must be open and not defensive when the program is criticized. But this does not mean abandoning the goals and vision inherent in the program.

One way to provide for input is to develop response sheets for those who have participated in the program. Certainly there should be an opportunity for deeper reflection at the end of the curriculum by an evaluation team. The response sheets, furthermore, should not be just for evaluation, but also for the first steps of what the parish will do afterwards. Since the entire curriculum is presented as a beginning of understanding, not a final answer, some of the questions can lead onward toward what parishioners would like to see in the future.

IV. REAPING THE HARVEST

One of the goals of a curriculum that is homegrown is that there will be a niche for everyone in a parish. That is, enough different ideas and programs will be developed so that people of many interests and talents will want to become involved. The same goes for the follow-up to the curriculum and its attendant activities. Some people will be interested in continuing some form of direct service with the poor in the community. Others will want to work on public policy issues with such groups as Impact and Bread for the World. Some will choose to support the programs of the Presiding Bishop's Fund, CROP or Oxfam-America. Still other routes could be through additional educational efforts, a food co-op, nutrition programs or examination of food programs that operate locally.

Each parish will have to evaluate its own particular course. But it is to be hoped that the curriculum will have helped the parish to see that there is much that can be done in feeding the hungry, in helping the hungry to feed themselves, and that the issue is one of long-term concern. This last point is critical. If the program succeeds, at least part of the success will be that it spurs people to accept the responsibility as Christians to be intimately involved in the needs of their hungry neighbors.

In many ways the faces of the hungry today are a challenge to affluent Christians. It challenges them to choose between their relative comfort and the risks of caring and even sacrificing for others. In effect, the challenge of world hunger is that the people who take the name of Jesus Christ as their own need to make that commitment real and visible in the world today. The harvest that we shall see is that of the hungry able to feed themselves and the faces of children rising out of poverty into a fuller life. It is the harvest of those who dare to witness to the coming of a new Kingdom.

BIBLIOGRAPHY

Collins, Joseph, and Lappé, Francis Moore. *Food First.* Boston: Houghton Mifflin, 1977. This is perhaps the most detailed single study on world hunger. The book has generated controversy with its assertion that the world could feed itself if there were significant social, political, and economic changes. The format is based on response to often-asked questions. Readable and challenging.

CROP Resource Packet and *CROP Crossroads.* Elkhart, Indiana: CROP. CROP, the national hunger appeal of Church World Service, has developed several valuable resource packets for local use. These provide brief essays on hunger questions, film lists, worship ideas, and other valuable tools.

Freudenberger, C. Dean, and Minus, Paul. *Christian Responsibility in a Hungry World.* Nashville: Abingdon, 1976. A brief, readable introduction to the hunger issue. It includes some good suggestions for responses by churches.

Hunger on Spaceship Earth ($2.50 plus 35¢ postage from American Friends Service Committee, 15 Rutherford Pl, New York, New York, 10003). A packet for hunger programs that includes short articles, a simulation game, graphs, and other usable educational tools. It has some short essays that have a witty reflection on American life-styles.

Katz, Deborah, and Goodwin, Mary. *Food: Where Nutrition, Politics and Culture Meet* ($4.50 from Center for Science in the Public Interest,

1755 S Street NW, Washington, D. C. 20009). This book not only contains numerous ideas on nutrition education, it also has some of the most creative activities for groups imaginable. It includes detailed information on diet and consumption as well as facts on farm and food policies.

Kutzer, Patricia, and Sullivan, Timothy. *Who's Involved in Hunger* ($1.00 from American Freedom from Hunger Foundation, 1625 Eye Street NW, Washington D. C. 20006 or World Hunger Education Service, 245 Second Street NE, Washington, D. C. 20002). A short guide to organizations doing different programs and with varied resources in world hunger areas.

Sidec, Ronald. *Rich Christians in an Age of Hunger*. Downers Grove, Ill.: Inter-Varsity Press, 1977. The best biblical examination of Christian involvement in world hunger. Takes a strong position on discipleship and life-style, as well as a hard-nosed analysis of present relations between the rich and poor. The book is a challenge to a full and deep response by Christians to the needs of the hungry and God's demands for justice.

Simon, Arthur. *Bread for the World.* New York: Paulist Press, and Grand Rapids: Eerdmans, 1975. The "original" introduction to the hunger issue by the president of Bread for the World. It provides brief background chapters on hunger and the church and maps out responses, especially in the area of public policy.

Taylor, J. V. *Enough is Enough.* London: SCM Press, 1975. A simple yet profound essay on Christian life-style in a hungry world. It has a warm sense of gently calling for a new way of living without a threatening or demeaning condemnation of present excesses.

·11·

The Language of Theology

JOSEPH P. RUSSELL

We have a natural need to describe our experiences and relate the story of our lives. But there are some aspects of our experiences that are impossible to describe with precision—the love that we feel for spouse, family, and friends, for example—so we express these experiences with symbol language, poetry, or analogy in order to share our feelings with each other. "Love comforteth like sunshine after rain" (Shakespeare). The writer gropes for images or pictures that can communicate the great joy that is felt. Great symphonies, works of art, and literary masterpieces have all stemmed from the urge to communicate what is beautiful, all-encompassing, and beyond easy description.

Such language must communicate the unique feelings of the writer or speaker in such a way that it enables the hearer to respond to the image and join his or her imagination with that of the speaker. If the imagery is to communicate, it must provide a picture that allows enough room for the hearer to add to and expand the poetry as the experience is interpreted and adapted.

To describe God is the supreme task of every culture and people. Even the person busily denying the presence of a god is still forced to come to terms with some ultimate questions about life and death, meaning and purpose. (I can still remember a conversation my son had with his friend when he was in the second grade. "There is no God," the friend, who was the child of atheist parents, said with conviction. "Well, then, what makes things grow?" my son asked.

"Why, Mother Nature, of course," the friend replied confidently. In responding to the "why" questions of their son, the parents had been forced to use "god language" to explain the ultimate questions of life.)

The language of theology, like the language of the lover, is the language of poetry, analogy, and imagery. Like the lover's description, the theologian must use images that convey common meanings and yet do not limit the hearers' search for their own sense of truth. Jesus' parables are perfect examples of this theological approach. "The Kingdom of God is like a mustard seed," Jesus said. This image, like the Kingdom it describes, never stops growing as the hearer meditates on the simple truth conveyed in the imagery.

The Gospels of Matthew, Mark, and Luke tell the story of Jesus and draw some reflections and conclusions from those events, as mentioned in the first chapter of this book. But the Gospel of John goes one step further. The writer of this Gospel provides us with a poetic theology that interprets the events of Jesus' life, death, and resurrection for the growing church. Compare the birth narrative of the second chapter of Luke with the poetic interpretation of that story in the first chapter of John. Compare the simple feeding story in Mark 6:30–44 with the interpretaton of that story in the sixth chapter of John.

The writer of John used rich imagery to convey the impact of the Risen Christ on the church. Jesus is the "Good Shepherd, the living water, the bread of life, the light of the world, the resurrection, the light, the Way, the Truth and the Life." These rich and beautiful images, like the parables of Jesus, grow ever deeper in the consciousness of anyone who meditates on them. The language of theology is a growing and nurturing language. The moment it becomes restrictive and definitive, it moves from theology to dogma and doctrine. The function of doctrine is to protect the institution that promulgates it. The function of theological language and imagery is to lead the faith seeker into deeper truth about God and the relationship of creation to creator.

To convey deep truths that are beyond our comprehension, we define the truth by enclosing it in a systematic structure that *is* comprehensible. Like the laboratory researcher who examines the pattern of one species of life in order to approach a study of the larger life systems, so the theologian recalls and examines a definitive story in order to approach an understanding of an indefinite, undefinable mystery. As Christians we believe that

God reveals the mystery of his power in the story of his people and most of all in the story of Jesus of Nazareth. But the story is not a closed entity. The story that can be told, celebrated, and dramatized is simply the window through which we view the incomprehensible mystery of God's creative power that lies beyond any story, poetry, or definition.

Let's look at the Nicene Creed from this perspective. We know that God does not live "up there" and that Jesus did not "descend" and then "ascend" into the heavens. Such wording predates space travel and an awareness of "out there" rather than "up" and "down." To say that Jesus "is seated at the right hand of the Father" is to paint a literal picture of a son seated by a father in some heavenly throne room. The Nicene Creed expresses Christian truth through the eyes of fourth-century theologians who conceived of a simple world where God did indeed dwell above the clouds and sky in heaven.

So what is the point of such outdated imagery? The vivid imagery of the Nicene Creed provides us with a closed and simplistic framework out of which we can search for our understanding of the mystery of God's direct action in our lives. There is a creative and mysterious power, the Creed states, that is the source of all creation, "of all that is seen and unseen." We call this creative power "Father," to denote a personal relationship. But this "Father" is more than creator. "He"—and that pronoun, too, is drawn from the imagery of the theological system expressed by the Creed—is directly involved in the life of every person. He identifies personally with the struggle of his people. He is known intimately and creatively in the flesh and blood of the struggle toward wholeness of his people.

The mercy and healing love of this creative power was uniquely revealed through the man Jesus who was "crucified under Pontius Pilate . . . suffered death and was buried. On the third day he rose again in accordance with the Scriptures. . . ." The fantastic realization that came through the life, death, and resurrection of Jesus of Nazareth leads the Christian to feel the intimate presence of God in every moment of life, suffering, promise, and hope. This understanding of God's presence, we call "the Son."

The Creed goes on to describe the role of the Holy Spirit, "the

Lord, the giver of life." After the resurrection of Jesus, the Apostles discovered that the power of Jesus to heal and proclaim the Lord's presence was within them. They were inspired or filled with the Spirit of God and enabled to act in God's name. In secular language, we may say that we feel inspired or "turned on" or filled with the spirit. In Christian theological language we speak of being filled with the Holy Spirit and "lifted up" into the presence of God.

Creedal statements are not meant to limit truth to literal interpretations of fact. They are meant to be launching devices into an ever-evolving understanding of truth and wonder. We accept the Creed or story as a statement of the whole truth, but in fact the creed and story point to the truths as yet to be revealed in time and eternity. The moment we have literally codified a body of knowledge about God in our minds, we have lost our sense of mystery and wonder of creation and God's place in it. The Nicene Creed provides us with a simplistic framework of a father in heaven, a son at his right side and the Holy Spirit who "proceeds from the Father and the Son" so that we can begin to apprehend something of the wonder of our intimate relationship with the creative energy we dare to address as parent, sibling, spirit within.

The simplest and earliest creed of the church may have been the simple statement found in some Western texts of the eighth chapter of the Book of Acts. "I believe that Jesus Christ is the son of God" (*Interpreter's Bible,* Vol. 9, p. 116). Even this simple statement builds a framework of imagery in order to express the inexpressible. The term "Son of God" had deep symbolic connotations for the Jews and early Christians. This imagery helped to convey the kind of relationship the people felt for the risen Christ.

The "Creed" of the Old Testament is found in Deuteronomy, chapter 26. The Israelites were to come before the priest at the Temple with their first fruit offerings and recite their common story. "My father was a wandering Aramean who went down to Egypt with a small household and lived there as an alien . . . we cried to the Lord, the God of our Fathers, and he heard our cry and saw our affliction, our toil and our oppression. He brought us out of Egypt with his strong hand and outstretched arm. . . ." This statement of belief in the power of God revealed through the story of his people led the Israelite to the further recitation of the "Shema" or statement of faith in the one God. "Hear, O Israel! The Lord is our God, the Lord alone" (Deut. 6:4).

Notice that both Old and New Testament "creeds" provide a story as the framework for understanding the mysterious and awesome presence of God. The story becomes the framework out of which the theology is built. By understanding how God was revealed to the Israelites in the wilderness, every generation of Jewish people understands the action of God in their lives. By understanding how God was revealed through the life, death, and resurrection of Jesus of Nazareth, the Christian understands how God is revealing himself in the "flesh and blood" of every believer's life. God's mysterious power is conveyed through the story. A person who sees God's presence revealed in the midst of the worst suffering will not lose hope. Even the gas ovens of Nazi Germany could not destroy the will of a people. The same event of terror and tragedy may well destroy the will of a person who cannot apprehend meaning to her struggle in life. The language and simplistic structures of theological language are extremely important. As noted above, they provide the window through which we sense the revelation of creative power in our lives and in eternity.

The prayer of consecration that forms the central statement of Christian worship rehearses the story of all creation and specifically of Jesus. Christians hear this story rehearsed at every celebration of the Eucharist in capsulated form. Out of this very simple story of creation, fall, birth, life, death, and resurrection, the Christian comprehends the action of God in all life and creation at all time.

In the story of our people as they struggled across the wilderness and began to comprehend the signs of God's power, we understand God's power in our struggle through the wilderness and discovery times of our pilgrimage. In the story of the man Jesus, we accept the clearest statement of God's action in our life, world, and universe. No wonder we tell, sing, dramatize, and respond to the story of our people.

Our prayer life is centered upon this same "story" language and framework. We address "Our father in heaven" and feel in touch with a personal creative power because the simple, understandable title of "father" provides a window through which we can search the vast stretches of mystery and address the power that is becoming in each one of us.

In our search for knowledge we tend to feel uncomfortable unless we can prove something scientifically. Generations of scholars have set out to prove the existence of the historical Jesus or the activity of God in the world. But actually much of scientific truth is postulated on the same kind of "creedal" statements as religious truths are. In order to study or understand the mysteries of science, it is often necessary to make definitive statements about undefinable mysteries. These definitive statements form the basis for the study and for coming to deeper understandings of the problems being examined. When there is a new break-through in scientific discovery, it is sometimes necessary to completely change the definitive statements to fit the new discoveries.

Sometimes the changes in definitive statements are agreed upon; for example, we are now facing the shock of defining distance in meters and kilometers rather than in feet or miles. But until I have some feel for what a kilometer is, my distance perspective on the freeway is going to be distorted. The highway department helps by posting both mileage and kilometer signs for me so that I can slowly grow into the new language. The signposts for our understanding of God's action in our life is the story of our people as revealed in the Bible. In designing and developing our homegrown programs, we need to help each other use and understand the language of religion and theology, and the first step in this process is to make sure that our people are aware of their definitive story as it is revealed in the Bible. This process needs to be at the heart of any program.

We may also find it helpful to provide people with a double set of signs along the pilgrim's way in understanding theology. Step out of the Christian story for a while and live in a completely different "story" definition of reality. Then lead the people back across the threshold into the Christian story again. Through the process of parallel journeys, we discover in a renewing way the power of our own story. My feeling for what a mile involves in distance is heightened as I experience the parallel feeling of a kilometer.

For example, after the film *Star Wars* was shown at a local theater we could talk about "the force" and about God with some new understanding. *Star Wars* was no great theological breakthrough, but it did allow children and adults to experience a completely different understanding of reality and find some common ground as they returned to celebrate the "Christian force" the following Sunday.

The children's series written by C. S. Lewis is finding increasing popularity with persons of all ages. There are seven books in the series beginning with *The Lion, The Witch and the Wardrobe.* The books issued in a paperback edition, are packaged together and sold under the title *The Chronicles of Narnia.* The lion Aslan is seen as the Christ figure in the series. The children, around whom the story centers, enter and leave the mysterious world of Narnia in strange and unforeseen ways. At the end of the adventures portrayed in *The Voyage of the Dawn Treader,* Aslan explains to Lucy and Edmund that in their world they will continue to know him by another name.

> "Please, Aslan," said Lucy. "Before we go, will you tell us when we can come back to Narnia again? Please. And oh, do, do, do make it soon."
>
> "Dearest," said Aslan very gently, "you and your brother will never come back to Narnia."
>
> "Oh, Aslan!" said Edmund and Lucy both together in despairing voices.
>
> "You are too old, children," said Aslan, "and you must begin to come close to your own world now."
>
> "It isn't Narnia, you know," sobbed Lucy. "It's *you.* We shan't meet *you* there. And how can we live, never meeting you?"
>
> "But you shall meet me, dear one," said Aslan.
>
> "Are—are you there too, Sir?" said Edmund.
>
> "I am," said Aslan. "But there I have another name. You must learn to know me by that name. This was the very reason why you were brought to Narnia, that by knowing me here for a little, you may know me better there."

C. S. Lewis explained to his young readers that by reading the stories of Narnia, they would understand the story of Christ more fully. They would know his presence in their lives better because they had seen the world of Narnia through the eyes of Aslan's story of creation, fall, and redemption. Now those familiar Christian terms take on new meaning as they are expressed in a completely different setting.

Works of fantasy are becoming increasingly popular. Some see fantasy as an escape from reality, but I see fantasy as a very valid way to come to a deeper understanding of truth as it is revealed through the Bible. The old reruns of "Star Trek" episodes have generated faithful followers who call themselves "Trekkies." The works of Tolkein, Ursula LeGuin, and Madeleine L'Engle listed in the bibliography of this chapter are familiar to many.

In the Diocese of Oregon we have designed several intergenerational camps based on two of C. S. Lewis's books, Brian Hall's *Nog's Vision,* and Trina Paulus' *Hope for the Flowers* (see bibliography). Our camps have been held over three-day summer weekends. As people arrived at the conference site, they were led into an experience of living in the fantasyland revealed by *Nog's Vision.* The world portrayed here is one where the creatures, called Pricklies, were ruled totally by the work ethic until the birth of a strange blue "non-Prickly" called Nog. He brought laughter to the people and allowed them to see the vision of their inner selves. On the first day at camp, adults and children recreated the land of the Pricklies. They accomplished ridiculous tasks and were kept very busy in our simulation of life in Prickly City. Nog arrived in time to offer us a night of laughter, dancing, and appreciation of a new world of dreams and visions. The following day produced an "Olymprics" field day with games and contests for everyone. We worshiped, played, did KP, danced, and laughed in the new idiom of Prickly City. A "theology" of Prickly City developed as we experienced the life in the reality of Pricklies. At the end of the weekend, we began the process of translating our Prickly City reality into the language, experience, and world-view of the Christian story.

In simulating life "before" and "after" in Prickly City we helped each other define the truth of the Pricklies' world. How did they understand their lives and find meaning? What happened to change their reality? What new world-view came to the Pricklies after the birth of Nog? What creeds might they have written? What prayers would they have said at their birth, crises, and at death? What hopes and thanksgivings guided them in their struggle for understanding and wholeness?

The same kinds of questions need to be asked as we enter into any "story system" of study. Children love to read or hear the C. S. Lewis stories. A class where the stories were shared would become a religious education experience as the participants were led to reflect on the questions the adventurers raised about life. We don't want to destroy the story by analyzing it, but we can raise questions that help participants think theologically about the story world of Narnia and about their own world and lives.

In a vacation church school setting we helped children experience the world of the Hebrews as they followed Moses out of Egypt, through the wilderness, and into the Promised Land. We spent four hours a day for five days in a city park dramatizing the Exodus story and helping the children feel the experiences of their people. Through that process of experiencing the world of the people of the story we could begin the important process of reflection. How did our people understand God? How did they understand their relationship with God? If we accept reality through the framework of this central story in our faith, what does the story say about our understanding of God? The details of this experience are published in the resource *Adventures in Exodus: Our Quest for Freedom* (see bibliography).

The next summer we focused on the life of Jesus in the same way as we told the stories he told and recalled the acts of his life. The same kind of reflection process followed the simulation of the story.

Theology is a rather awesome word and, as I mentioned in chapter one ("The Bible and Religious Education"), we tend to think of theologians as being scholars, writers, and seminary professors. But to think theologically is the goal we must all have as religious educators. Helping persons to reflect on the stories that shape our understanding of God's action in our lives and then reflecting on how we see God acting in our own life and times is the primary purpose of our homegrown religious education programs. Out of this reflection comes our commitment to the One God of our foreparents, and to Jesus Christ as Lord and Savior.

Children love to play, and so do adults. I think that through play we can discover truth. Watch young children play house together. You can learn more about how they perceive their own family structure than in hours of talking. Sometimes their perception of us as parents is a bit shattering! The children are not only reflecting how they see their family structure, but they are also trying on different roles within the family. Playing becomes learning for them. This is the role of the simulation games that are used extensively in public education these days. Everything from playing Monopoly to simulating life in the wilderness with Moses can become a play experience that leads to a deepening understanding of faith and commitment. What moves the experience from play to education is the reflection that goes with the process. Players become theologians as they begin to comprehend the mysteries of life, creation, and eternity through the window of the story they have just experienced together.

Getting participants to express their story-experience in poetry, symbol, and drama is the next step. In the twelfth chapter of Exodus, the Jewish people are called to dramatize the experience of their foreparents, as they are to this day. In a sense, the festival of Passover is a "simulation game" centered around a meal that the whole Jewish people participates in annually. (We can make the same point about Christian liturgy. We simulate the Last Supper so that we can participate directly in the experience of being fed by Jesus.) Psalm 136 expresses the story in an extended litany that recalls the mighty acts of God in the history of our people. As each event is rehearsed before the people, they respond "for his mercy endures forever." The rehearsal of the story becomes a chant of responsive praise, and the people become caught up in the act of recalling almost in the way the crowd at the football game gets caught up in the spirit of the game through the chants of the cheerleaders. In this kind of powerful reenactment of the story, the people of every generation begin to feel the power of participating in the story of their foreparents. Poetry is another powerful way of expressing the reflections that arise out of the experience.

To tie the thoughts of this chapter together, I want to share the outline of a retreat we designed for children in the fifth through the ninth grade several years ago.

DOING THEOLOGY
A WEEKEND RETREAT FOR YOUTH

Purpose: To enable participants to share an experience together and to reflect on that experience as a means of apprehending truth about themselves, their world, and their relationship with each other and with their Creator. To encourage participants to express the truths they have discovered in symbol, ritual, and word.

SESSION ONE (Saturday morning)

Purpose: To talk about community and to enable participants to experience a sense of community.

Reflections on the design: After introduction to each other and to the weekend plans, we talked about the meaning of community. The "ingredients" of community were discussed. People who share a common story or experience feel a part of a community, as well as people who work together, live together, share the same ideals, and so forth. We also talked about the feelings of being alone and isolated. Jesus and the disciples at the Last Supper were used as an example of community. The disciples' sense of aloneness at the time of the crucifixion was our example of aloneness or separation.

Points in the design: Participants were asked to spend five minutes alone. They were asked to close their eyes and experience the sense of being completely alone and separate. We then brought the participants back together and taught them a simple folk dance, using music from *Zorba the Greek.* This was followed by the "trust walk," in which one person guided a partner who was blindfolded. Partners then switched roles. The guide was asked to lead his partner in various experiences of walking, drinking water, sitting down, and so forth. Following these three experiences, we brought the participants back together for a reflection time. As a part of the reflection we talked about the importance of trust in building community. The disciples had trust in Jesus to heal and guide them. They trusted each other in the common sharing that they experienced together with Jesus.

SESSION TWO (Saturday afternoon)

Purpose: To share a common experience together and to reflect on the implications of that experience.

Reflections on the design: Our understanding of how God touches our lives comes out of the story of the Israelites of the Old Testament and Jesus and the Apostles of the New Testament. As our people reflected on their experiences together they saw the revelation of God acting in their story. God had revealed himself and his will and dream of wholeness for them. This story of our people shapes our understanding of how God is working in our story. These stories are the windows through which we view reality, meaning, suffering, and hope.

To come to a deeper understanding of how theology happens among a people, we asked the children to enter a whole new world and understanding. For two hours we asked the participants to pretend they were discovering their world for the first time.

Points in the design: Participants were divided into groups of from ten to twelve with two adult leaders assigned to each group. We separated the groups by sending them to completely different areas of the conference center. The leaders were ceremoniously presented with sealed instructions as they left for their area. As they arrived at their assigned point, the leader opened the mysterious envelope and read aloud the following secret instructions:

INSTRUCTIONS FOR COMMUNITY GROUPS

Something has happened to each of you so that you all soon will have total and complete amnesia. You will become aware that you are together, but you will have absolutely no idea of who you are, where you came from, what you are doing together or what lies over the next hill. For all you know, the world might end over that hill or you might be the only beings in this strange place. *In sum, the only thing you will know is what you will experience together.* After reading this message all memories of the past will leave you. It may even be that you will have to develop a new language! Can you understand each other? Because you don't know anything about the world around you it will be necessary to discover everything for the first time. How does one get out of this building? What is that big light away up in the sky? What is that sound? Flowing water—where does it come from?

After you have made some discoveries and perhaps found that you can all understand the same sound symbols (language) you might begin to wonder as a group:

- Where have we come from?
- What are we doing here? Is there any reason for our being here? Where are we going? Are there others like us somewhere?
- Are we afraid of anything? What if we meet other beings like us—will they be friendly—will they hurt us?

You may want to do some exploring as a group. But be careful!

The world just might end over that next hill or outside that door and you could fall down into a bottomless pit!

How are you going to get along together? Will you make rules to live by? Will you have leaders and divide up the work between you? If you meet other beings, will you try to bring them into your community or will you keep them away from you?

Who or what put us here? Where does our life come from? Is there a source for all that is around us? What makes the water flow and from where does it come? If something put us here is It or He or She watching us now? Had we better do something to make this Power happy with us? If it put us here, it might destroy us just as quickly! Does this mysterious force have the power to guide us, or help us, or save us from some of the things we are frightened of? If it does, we had better listen to it. Can this power talk to us? Maybe it's speaking to us through the sounds of the brook. Maybe the clouds are saying something to us.

You have finished reading this message. Now all memory of the past is leaving you . . . all memory is gone . . .

The groups then spent the next two hours in the simulation experience. We held our breath wondering if they would be willing to live in the situation and were pleased to discover how easily everyone adapted, including the adult leaders. One of the adults brought her very young child, and the child enhanced the experience for the whole group as they had to include caring for and about the child in discovering their world and reality. At periods during the afternoon the leaders helped the group reflect on the questions raised in the secret instructions.

The simulation ended as we brought the participants back into the "real world" and asked them to share their experiences.

SESSION THREE (Sunday morning)

Purpose: To encourage participants to move from the reflection of their experience to the expression of it in symbol, ritual, and word.

Reflections on design: If the experience is to have power in the lives of the people, it must be recalled, reexperienced and expressed so that it is continually reinforced in the lives of the people.

The Sacraments of the church, the hymns, poems, and creeds that we share together, the stories that we hand on to the next generation, are all ways that we reinforce the reflections of our experiences and find common power in them. In this session we wanted to give the participants some direct experience in expressing their own reflections, their own theology of yesterday's story.

Points in the design: The groups met again in their own special areas after being sent forth with a ceremony. This time they were commissioned, as were the Apostles of Jesus, to go out and share with others their experience of truth and community discovered the day before. How is the group going to reinforce its discovery of truth? How will they pass their story on to future generations? If others are to be included in their community, how will they be brought in and made to feel a part of the total experience of the group? This afternoon, we told each group, you will be asked to include the rest of us in your experience. How will you do it in symbol, ritual, and word?

SESSION FOUR (Sunday afternoon)

Purpose: To share an experience of symbol, ritual, and word that expresses truth and power for the participants.

Reflections on design: Acts 10:34–48 describes Peter's address to the pagan family of Cornelius. Peter rehearsed for Cornelius and his family the mighty acts of Jesus, beginning with his baptism. Following the sharing of that experience, the pagans received the power of the Holy Spirit. Through the hearing of the story, the pagans were open to the power of God in their lives too. We might say that their eyes were open to a whole new reality in their lives and in their world. They were now filled with the Holy Spirit. Peter then "gave orders for them to be baptised in the name of Jesus Christ" (Acts 10:48; Jerusalem Bible).

This story of Peter and Cornelius formed the basis of our afternoon experience of story, symbol, and ritual sharing.

Points in design: All the participants met together after lunch. We formed a procession and moved to the first group area. The members of the group shared with us their story of yesterday. Woven into their narrative was their "theology." We heard some adventure stories that day. We also shared in those adventures in the way they were told and in the way that they were received. Then each of us was "baptized" into the community that had shared its experience with us. We were anointed with water, hugged, given flowers, and loved, invited and empowered in all kinds of ways that afternoon. I shall never forget this day. The Sacraments were offered in new forms and new expressions and the creeds spoke of clouds and flowing waters, but as the afternoon unfolded a new awareness of the Holy Spirit and God's eternal presence in every form and in every story became clearer.

SESSION FIVE (Midafternoon Sunday)

Purpose: To proclaim our Christian story, our commonly held reflections of that story (theology), and to celebrate and be empowered by that story in symbol, ritual, and word.

Reflections on design: We could now talk about the Judaic/Christian story with a new awareness of how theology happens among a people. God reveals himself in the lives of his people. That revelation becomes clear as we reflect and celebrate the story. And now that we perceive God's presence in the world, the Holy Spirit can empower us to act in God's name, to love, to heal, and to proclaim hope in God's world. The story out of which this awareness comes is our "window" to the incomprehensible mystery of creation and creative power. The story gives us a handle, a sense of relationship to the mystery. "Therefore we proclaim the mystery of faith: Christ has died. Christ has risen. Christ will come again" (Proposed Book of Common Prayer, p. 363).

Points in design: Using "An Order for Celebrating the Holy Eucharist" (Proposed Book of Common Prayer, p. 400) as the basis for our celebration, we gave each group a portion of the liturgy to design and offer. For example, one of the groups was asked to help us "Gather in the Lord's Name." They had to decide where we would have our celebration and what the environment would be. They included some of the symbols shared by each group earlier in the afternoon along with the Christian symbols that we were all familiar with. The second group was asked to help us "Proclaim and Respond to the Word of God." What Bible readings would express our life together this weekend? Could they adapt some of the words shared earlier this day into our celebration of the Word of God? The "sermon" in this celebration was simply the reflections of priest and people.

Another group offered the prayers "for the World and the Church," and another group "Prepared the Table" and the elements of the Eucharist.

This is not meant to be a complete design but is simply offered as an example of the kind of homegrown program that can be designed as you think about the theology of your own lives. I believe that theology is everyone's responsibility as Christians. When we recall the excitement that our biblical foreparents felt in discovering and reflecting on God's presence in their lives, we can sense the joy of being "theologians." May people say of us we feel the excitement of God's spirit filling us in their stories, "Everyone was amazed and unable to explain it; they asked one another what it all meant. Some, however, laughed it off. 'They have been drinking too much new wine,' they said" (Acts 2:12–13).

This is the kind of responsive joy that we too can know as we see through the window of our stories the reality of God calling us all into the eternal mystery of ever-unfolding creation.

BIBIOGRAPHY

Crossan, John Dominic. *The Dark Interval: Towards a Theology of Story.* Niles, Ill.: Argus Communications, 1975.

Keen, Sam, and Fox, Anne Valley. *Telling Your Story: A Guide to Who You Are and Who You Can Be.* New York: Signet, New American Library, 1973.

The Keen and Crossan books provide guidelines for helping us share our own personal stories. They would be helpful in guiding persons in seeing theological implications in their lives.

Hall, Brian. *Nog's Vision.* New York: Paulist Press, 1975.

L'Engle, Madeleine. *The Irrational Season.* New York: Seabury Press, 1977.

Lewis, C. S. *The Lion, The Witch and the Wardrobe; Prince Caspian; The Voyage of the Dawn Treader; The Silver Chair; The Horse and His Boy; The Magician's Neptune; The Last Battle.* New York: Collier Books, 1970. The significance of this series is stated in the body of the chapter.

McClendon, James William, Jr. *Biography as Theology: How Life Stories Can Remake Today's Theology.* Nashville, Tenn.: Abingdon Press, 1974. An excellent book that helps us to see the power behind the story as it shapes the understanding of each person McClendon traces in his book. Our "world-view" comes out of how we perceive our story. This becomes our theology of life and action.

Paulus, Trina. *Hope for the Flowers.* New York: Paulist Press, 1972.

Russell, Joseph P., et al. *Adventures in Exodus: Our Quest for Freedom.* New York: The Seabury Press, rev. 1975. We designated a curriculum based on the Exodus experience that helps participants experience the concepts of the Exodus story. The curriculum deals with our quest for freedom and liberation. Our design grew out of a summer park day-camping experience, but the curriculum can be adapted for other settings.

Sawyer, Ruth. *The Way of the Storyteller.* New York: Penguin Books, 1970.

John and Mary Harrell recommend this book and *The Art of Story Telling* to those interested in learing and practicing the art.

Shedlock, Marie L. *The Art of the Story Teller.* New York: Dover Publications, 1951.

Sloyan, Virginia, ed. *Signs, Songs and Stories: Another Look at Children's Liturgies.* Washington, D.C.: The Liturgical Conference, 1974. This is another good resource book for the liturgist/educator. We can see how the story fits into the liturgical context.

Westerhoff, John H. *Will Our Children Have Faith?* New York: Seabury Press, 1976. A very beautiful book that calls into question some of the assumptions that we make about religious education. These he proposes to replace with a community-of-faith-enculturation method in which the community of faith is the context and interactions between generations are the means of education. The nature of a faith community, the importance of ritual, tradition, experience in the community, and community acts in the world are evaluated.

BV 1471.2 .H64 1979
790732

Homegrown Christian
education